The Weiser Field Guide to
witches

The Weiser Field Guide to
witches

From Hexes to Hermione Granger,
from Salem to the Land of Oz

Judika Illes

WEISERBOOKS
San Francisco, CA/Newburyport, MA

First published in 2010 by
Red Wheel/Weiser, llc
With offices at:
500 Third Street, Suite 230
San Francisco, CA 94107
www.redwheelweiser.com

ISBN: 978-1-57863-479-8

Library of Congress Cataloging-in-Publication Data
is available upon request.

Typeset in Adobe Jenson and Priori Sans

Cover photograph © Vintage Images/Hulton Archive/
Getty Images. Images on p 5, 6, 9, 15, 17, 18, 23, 24, 29, 35, 36,
43, 50, 55, 58, 61, 64, 71, 78, 82, 87, 93, 95, 99, 101, 103,
105, 108, 110, 114, 116, 126, 134, 140, 148, 154, 162, 169, 176,
179, 180, 185, 187, 188, 206, 208, 218, 227, 228, 241, 244,
249, 254, 262 © dreamstime.com; images on p 33, 38, 98, 190,
198 © istockphoto.com, images on p 52, 223, 225, 232, 247
© Pepin Press, images on p 19, 26, 30, 46, 73, 90, 111, 122, 128,
137, 175, 217, 235, 237, 243, 261, 265 © Miss Mary.

Printed in Canada
TCP
10 9 8 7 6 5 4 3 2 1

The paper used in this publication meets the minimum require-
ments of the American National Standard for Information
Sciences—Permanence of Paper for Printed Library Materials
Z39.48-1992 (R1997).

Contents

Introduction

Witches call to us from thresholds, crossroads, sea-shores, swamps, and mountain tops. Fairy-tale witches beckon from within wild forests. Urban witches mingle in stores stocked with candles, crystals, statues, and mysterious books. Witches fly through the air and dig twisted roots from the ground.

Beautiful witches dance beneath the stars. Robed magicians chant in arcane tongues. Alluring witches ensorcell with the power of potions. Cadaverous hags stir steaming cauldrons. Flower- and pentacle-bedecked witches celebrate the seasons. Hideous witches lurk in horror films, working their wiles and *definitely* up to no good.

Witches peep out of greeting cards. They appear in advertising for hosiery, alcoholic beverages, and sandwich meat. They commandeer the pages of comic books, appearing in the guise of both villain and heroine. Witches consistently steal the show in movies and television, whether live-action or animated.

The obviously witchy dress in black and wear peaked hats. Other witches remain resolutely discreet, appearing totally ordinary and nondescript: nothing about their appearance reveals that they are witches. Witches gather herbs, draw down the moon, roll in morning dew, commune with animal familiars, perform magical feats and miracles of healing, live harmoniously with nature, and impose their will upon others. Witches hex, bless, curse, and remove curses cast by others.

So, what exactly is a witch? How can you recognize one? Is it possible that you *are* one?

A field guide is a book intended to help readers identify living beings or objects of natural occurrence (sea shells, for example). This may be a straightforward task when it comes to identifying butterflies or wild flowers, but witches are another story. Witches defy simple classification.

Since the earliest days of humanity, witches have been admired, adored, loved, feared, trusted, mistrusted, loathed, persecuted, killed, lusted after, and worshipped. Every culture around the world acknowledges the existence of witches, or at the very least recognizes some kind of witch. Witches inspire, in one form or another, every creative art: theater, music, paintings, dance, cinema, television, literature, and so forth. Witches appear in the most ancient myths and folklore. As brand new forms of entertainment, such as video games, emerge, witches continue to make their presence felt.

As time marches on, witches are more prevalent, not less. Even so, attempts to define exactly who—or what—witches are consistently leads to confusion and impassioned argument. Although very many are convinced that they know the true definition of "witch," their many definitions contradict each others'. Part of the problem is that one little word—"witch"—has evolved into an umbrella term encompassing many different concepts.

A "witch" is commonly defined as someone who practices magical arts, a spell-caster, or occultist. Many understand "witch" to be a synonym for "magic user." Other synonyms include *enchantress, sorcerer* and *sorceress, wizard, magician, mage, magus,* and its feminine counterpart, *maga.* A host of comparable words exist in multitudes of languages.

The magical arts are a broad field, not restricted to the casting of spells. Historically, at one time or another, alchemists, astrologers, mediums, seers, and fortune-tellers have all been classified as witches, although some would object to this classification. Some people do not differentiate between shamans and witches; others do. Over the centuries, the term "witch" has also encompassed midwives, herbalists, and other traditional healers. Healing and midwifery were once perceived as magical professions even though they may not be perceived that way today.

Some consider devotees of the Wiccan religion to be witches, regardless of whether or not a particular individual casts spells. Some perceive witches as those who live harmoniously with Earth's natural rhythms and resent the automatic association of witches with the occult.

Yet according to still others, magic isn't what witches *do*; it's what they *are*. Some define witches as members of a special magical race living amongst humans. Witches may look like people, but that resemblance is only superficial. Witches have superpowers that are innate or inherited. These witches are commonly found in popular culture; the TV shows *Bewitched* and *Charmed* and the *Harry Potter* series spring to mind.

Although some people consider this type of witch sheer fantasy, others sincerely believe that they exist.

East Asian lore takes this concept one step further: just as some people possess superpowers, so do some animals. Certain animal species, especially cats, foxes, and snakes, may also produce witches. The truly powerful are shape-shifters who can convincingly assume human form.

These animal witches tend to be female, which underscores another common perception about witches. Many consider witches and women to be intrinsically linked, although whether positively or negatively so is in the eye of the beholder.

Some perceive any sexy woman to be a "witch"; she's literally *bewitching*. This might be meant as a compliment, but it could also be construed as a warning. At times when women's beauty was perceived as dangerous—and in some places today—alluring women have sometimes been accused of being witches. The roots of the practice of veiling women may lie in attempts to protect vulnerable men from witches' wicked wiles.

To some, the word "witch" is a compliment, a badge of honor. Witches are emblematic of a certain kind of innate female power. A "witchy woman" is a creative, confident, resilient, indefatigable woman, walking her own path, comfortable in her own skin, in control of her own sexuality, beholden to no one.

Yet to others, "witch" is a potent insult. The word is frequently used to describe a defiant woman, one who doesn't know "her place," as well as any mean-spirited, nasty woman, regardless of magical skill or power. Many perceive "witch" as but a rhyming synonym for "bitch." In the 1939 MGM movie musical *The Wizard of Oz*, actress Margaret Hamilton portrays two characters: the green-skinned, black-hatted, magical practitioner called the Wicked Witch of the West, and the despised spinster neighbor, Miss Gulch. Both characters are referred to as witches.

Although historically many have been falsely accused of being witches, in fact, witches *do* exist: many different kinds of witches. Yes, of course, there are folk-tale witches and fairy-tale witches, literary witches and Hollywood witches. But most especially, there are countless living, breathing witches who bear that title with pride.

That doesn't mean that witches are easily pigeonholed. Witches come in all shapes, sizes, ages, colors, ethnicities, and genders. Witches live in every community and around the world. Some follow ancient paths; others forge and pioneer brand new ways.

There are Luddite witches and techno-witches, witches who have emerged from the secrecy of the broom closet and witches who fiercely guard their privacy. Witches belong to every political party and subscribe to many political creeds, from the most liberal to the archconservative. Historically, there have been fascist witches, anarchist witches, and monarchist witches.

Witches observe many religions and walk many spiritual paths. Although many modern witches are Wiccans, others have no religious affiliation, considering themselves atheists or agnostics. Still others identify themselves as Pagans, Christians, Jews, Buddhists, Hindus, and virtually any other religion that can be named. Although many find the concept of Christian witches contradictory, others do not.

Witches cannot be identified solely by appearance. A witch costume (black dress, peaked hat and often a broom) has been among the most popular Halloween costumes for generations, yet many who don the garb of the witch on that holiday would laugh if it were suggested that they were witches.

What then, do witches have in common? Is there a common denominator that unites these diverse people? Is there something that is intrinsic to being a witch?

In fact, there is. Witches of all kinds certainly do share something in common. The clue to what they share is hidden in the word "witch" itself. Rather than by apparel or appearance, a witch's identity is defined by something within.

The English word *witch* derives from an Anglo-Saxon root word, *wicce* (feminine form) or *wicca* (masculine form), meaning "wise one." (The word *Wicca* derives from the same source.) Witchcraft is the craft of the wise. Witches are the wise ones; the ones who *know*. Witches are knowledge seekers.

To know is not the same as being smart or edu-cated. What witches possess or strive to attain is deep spiritual knowledge, the wisdom of Earth, sea, and stars. Witches are privy to Earth's secrets. They possess knowledge of traditional lore whose roots first emerged in the depths of time.

Words in many languages acknowledge this con-cept of the witch as someone who possesses deep knowledge. For example, *ved'ma*, a Russian word for "witch", translates as "one who knows." The Congolese word *nganga* is translated as "witch," although a more accurate translation might be "medium"; someone who serves as a bridge to the spirit world. This word derives from a Kikongo language root word meaning "knowl-edge" or "skill" but with the specific implication of spiritual and magical knowledge.

Basic, universal magical theory suggests that every-thing that exists exerts and radiates some type of magic power. Different species, individuals, things, colors, fragrances, and objects all radiate their own unique powers. (No, this has not been scientifically proven, but bear in mind that until the very end of the 19th century the existence of radioactivity was unproven and was, in fact, pooh-poohed by very many distinguished and educated scientists. Absence of proof is not proof of absence.) Although these powers may not be visible, physically tangible, or measurable by current scientific means, still they exist and may be manipulated for good or ill by those who know how. Witches are the ones who know how or who have the potential, capacity, or desire to learn.

Of course, this knowledge also explains the mistrust that so many bear toward witches. People are often uncomfortable with those who know more than they do, especially if that knowledge is powerful and difficult to access. Witches are repositories and guardians of occult knowledge. The word *occult* means "secret" or "hidden." Occult knowledge is buried treasure, humanity's secret heritage. For millennia, during certain historical periods and in many locales, those in positions of authority have attempted to control access to knowledge. Attempts were made to destroy or censor information, especially that of a spiritual or magical nature that was deemed inconvenient or that contradicted official teachings. These attempts were often successful: very little documented evidence now survives regarding the spiritual traditions of pre-Christian Europe or pre-Islamic Arabia, for instance.

One quality witches often share is a tendency to resent and resist any attempt to limit access to knowledge. Witches are the ones determined to know, regardless of rules or regulations. Despite centuries of terrible persecution, witches have preserved and transmitted sacred information, often orally to one another and often at great personal risk.

Another characteristic many witches share is comfort with the liminal. The word *liminal* derives from the Latin *limen*, or threshold. Liminal indicates the in-between: states that are simultaneously neither and both. Liminal space simultaneously divides and bridges two realities. Thus the shore divides land from sea and simultaneously connects them. The two liminal times of day, twilight and dawn, are neither night nor day and yet merge the energies of both. The standard opening line of central European fairy tales—the equivalent of "Once upon a time"—is "Once there was and once there wasn't . . .," indicating that the story about to be told exists in a liminal region. When you are kind of awake yet still partially asleep, you are in a liminal state. If you stand with one foot in water and one on dry land, you are standing in the liminal.

Witches thrive in the liminal zone. An old northern European nickname for witches is "hedge riders." Once upon a time, massive hedgerows divided villages from forests. Witches were believed to perch on these hedgerows, thus living simultaneously in the civilized world *and* in wild nature.

An American folk name for "witch" is "two-headed," as in a two-headed woman, a two-headed man, or a two-headed doctor (as in witch doctor or Voodoo doctor). The witch possesses two metaphorical heads because he or she lives in two worlds simultaneously: The mundane world *and* the magical world; The world of people *and* the world of spirits

Witches possess the skill, knowledge, and instincts to safely navigate these worlds. They serve as bridges and mediums. An individual witch may or may not possess this knowledge, but she or he possesses the power to access and assimilate it if needed or desired. Witches know the secrets of plants, animals, rocks, and other people. They understand the power projected by colors, numbers, and words. Witches can banish ghosts and welcome kind spirits. They can see the future in cards and see your past reflected in the palm of your hand.

The world of witches is filled with passion, magic, high spirits, and joy. It is a world where the sacred is ever-present, a world in which even the most mundane objects possess deep spiritual significance. The world of witches is a world of wonder in which every color, incident, creature, sight, or sound has some sort of magical import. A succinct definition comes from author Aline DeWinter, who writes, "A Witch is a person who sees everything as alive and powerful. We walk in a sacred manner and all of nature responds."

Although the history of witches is punctuated with tragedy, witches famously love to revel and have fun. So grab your field guide, and welcome to the world of witches—let's explore! Let's meet some of the world's most fascinating witches.

The Weiser Field Guide to Witches embraces a broad definition of witches with a primary focus on witches as practitioners of magic.

Just so that we are on the same page, in this book:

+ *Witch* refers to *any* type of witch, regardless of spiritual or religious affiliation.

- *Wicca* refers to the modern religion first formalized by Gerald Gardner in the 1950s.
- *Wiccan* refers to devotees of Wicca.
- *Vodou* refers to the African Diaspora spiritual tradition that arose in Haiti.
- *Voodoo* refers to Vodou-related magical traditions specific to New Orleans.

CHAPTER I

Types of Witches

What does a witch believe? What does a witch do?
The answers to those questions are extremely complex.
There are many ways to be a witch. Witches ply their
craft in many ways. There are *many* witchcraft traditions. It is virtually impossible to condense complex
belief systems into a few sentences, and so what follows
is but a brief sampling and should not be considered
definitive. Witchcraft is a fluid, vital art. Perhaps you,
too, possess a unique perspective on how to practice

witchcraft and will pioneer new ways and crafts.

Many people are perplexed by the differences between Wicca and witchcraft. Witchcraft is a broad term that encompasses many styles, perspectives, and practices. Wicca refers to a very specific spiritual tradition. One person may be both Wiccan and a witch, but not all witches are Wiccans and perhaps vice versa.

Among the crucial differences between Wicca and witchcraft is that most Wiccan traditions require initiation and thus direct transmission from one member to another. Self-initiation is a controversial topic within the Wiccan community. There is no concept of initiation in many traditional paths. It's not that it's not required; it doesn't exist. There is no hierarchy. Each witch is an independent practitioner on his or her own path.

Alexandrian Wicca

This tradition's name pays tribute to its founder, Alex Sanders, and also to the ancient library of Alexandria, Egypt, once the largest library in the world and a repository of sacred, mystical wisdom. Alexandrian Wicca was established in the United Kingdom in the 1960s.

Atheist Witches

As atheists, these witches do not acknowledge a Supreme Creator or the Wiccan conception of a Lord and Lady; but work their magic using Earth's natural powers and energies. Some may work with elemental spirits such as land spirits or fairies.

Cabot Tradition

This tradition, based on the teachings of Salem witch Laurie Cabot, emphasizes that witchcraft is a science, art, and religion. The Cabot Tradition also emphasizes psychic development.

Chaos Magic

There is no one specific school of Chaos Magic, also spelled Chaos Magick, nor do its practitioners adhere to one specific philosophy or spiritual tradition. Instead those who define themselves as chaos magicians share a certain attitude toward magic. Chaos Magic is defined as the primal creative force in the universe.

Chaos magicians learn and experiment with various magical techniques in order to tap into this underlying, primal, creative force in whatever ways work best and most effectively for them. Chaos Magic is influenced by the work of visionary artist and magician Austin Osman Spare, who wrote, "What is there to believe, but in Self?"

The Clan of
Tubal Cain

This tradition, founded by English witch Robert Cochrane, is based on practical traditional witchcraft, shamanism, Celtic mysticism, and Cochrane's interpretation of Druidry. The American branch of the Clan of Tubal Cain is known as the 1734 Tradition.

Dianic Wicca

Sometimes also called Wimmin's Religion, Dianic Wicca is a feminist spiritual tradition and the only form of witchcraft that is exclusively female. Women's rights and rites are combined in celebration of female divinity. The name of the tradition pays tribute to the Italian goddess, Diana. Among Dianic Wicca's founding mothers is author Z. Budapest, who formed the Susan B. Anthony Coven in Los Angeles on the Winter Solstice of 1971.

In 1975, Budapest self-published *The Feminist Book of Lights and Shadows*, a collection of rituals and spells that became the basic text of Dianic Wicca. It has since been republished as *The Holy Book of Women's Mysteries: Feminist Witchcraft, Goddess Rituals, Spellcasting and Other Womanly Arts....* Dianic Wicca may be considered similar in essence to the women's mystery traditions of ancient Rome.

Most Dianic covens are exclusively female.

Sybil Leek sometimes called her own tradition Dianic, but what she practiced was not the same as Dianic Wicca.

Faerie Witchcraft

This shamanic tradition involves actual interaction with fairies. Faerie witches, also spelled fairy witches, practice Earth-centered magic with emphasis on plant and animal familiars. Historically, many witches have worshipped and communed with fairies. In 1662, while being interrogated, Scottish witch Isobel Gowdie described her visits to the Fairy Queen. Similar testimony was given in French, Italian, and Hungarian witch trials.

Faerie Witchcraft is profoundly influenced by Scottish clergyman Reverend Robert Kirk's mysterious account of Fairyland, *The Secret Commonwealth of Elves, Fauns, and Fairies*, written in 1691 but not published until the early 19th century. Influential modern practitioners of Faerie Witchcraft include authors R. J. Stewart and Aline DeWinter. Faerie Witchcraft is not the same as Feri Tradition, nor is it the same as the various Wiccan traditions identified as Fairy Wicca.

Feri Tradition

This shamanic, ecstatic, initiatory, spiritual, and magical system, also sometimes spelled Fairy, Faery, or Faerie Tradition, began its modern incarnation in the 1940s when author, poet, and witch Victor Anderson (1917–2001) began initiations. Anderson is typically described as Feri's "founder," but he described himself as a transmitter of ancient information. Another branch of Feri Tradition is known as Vicia. Anderson taught that Feri Tradition derives originally from a primordial people who emerged from Africa thousands of years ago, the original fairies—although they are known by many other names in different cultures. Their teachings were transmitted orally over the generations.

Feri is an experiential tradition and various distinct Feri lineages and teachers now exist. Different lineages are influenced to different extents by different spiritual traditions including Celtic, Hawaiian, and Vodou. What most Feri practitioners share in common is direct personal interaction with spirits or deities. They do not subscribe to the Wiccan Rede (*Do what you will but harm none*); instead, each practitioner must take personal responsibility for her or his own actions.

Gardnerian Wicca

Gardnerian Wicca is the oldest, most formal modern Wiccan tradition. Based on the teachings and practices of Gerald Gardner (1884–1964), it is named "Gardnerian" in order to honor him but also to distinguish this tradition from older, less formalized traditions.

The term Gardnerian Wicca may originally have been coined by Robert Cochrane, who was not a fan of Gardner or of his tradition. Its standard text is *The Gardnerian Book of Shadows*, which Gardner co-authored with Diane Valiente. At the time of its writing, Valiente and Gardner believed that they were involved in the evolution of an old faith, not the creation of a new one. More information about this tradition is found in the discussion of Wicca on page 31.

Hedge Witchery

No initiation is necessary to be a hedge witch. Hedge witches are unaffiliated, solitary practitioners. The term "hedge witch" derives from "hedge rider" and similar northern European synonyms for witch. A hedge is a dense wall of bushes and other shrubbery. Once upon a time, large, dense hedgerows separated a village from surrounding forests. The hedge is a liminal zone, simultaneously a barrier and a threshold between the civilized world and wild nature. Witches were the hedge-riders who navigated this zone.

The modern term "hedge witch" is sometimes used as a synonym for "kitchen witch" or is intended to serve as an all-encompassing name for the large community of non-affiliated, non-initiated, non-Wiccan witches. The term "hedge witch," however, possesses shamanic undertones. By definition, a hedge rider or hedge witch travels between at least two worlds: the world of conventional reality and a spirit or afterlife realm.

Hereditary Witchcraft

By definition, a hereditary witch comes from a family in which at least one other person is or was a witch. Most hereditary witches derive from a lineage of witches; the trait is often passed down from parent to child, although sometimes generations are skipped. The term is also sometimes used by someone with one long-ago ancestor who was a witch or believed to be one. "Hereditary witch" is not a definitive term, and different people may interpret it in different ways. Some hereditary witches share traditions that are unique to their own families, but others do not. Fictional witches are very frequently hereditary; for instance, the Halliwell Sisters from the television series *Charmed*, or the Pure Bloods of the *Harry Potter* universe. Most modern witches are not hereditary.

Hoodoo

A high percentage of the enslaved Africans in the pre-Civil War United States were of Congolese origin. They brought a sophisticated system of magic with them to North America, where it merged with European folk magic, Native American, and other African traditions to form a whole new magical system now called Hoodoo. A practitioner of Hoodoo is traditionally known as a "worker." Hoodoo is very closely related to New Orleans Voodoo; the names are sometimes used interchangeably.

Hoodoo is a system of practical magic, not a specific spiritual tradition. Hoodoo practitioners may belong to any or no religion. There are Pagan, atheist, and Jewish Hoodoo workers, for instance. Some Hoodoo traditions are intensely Christian. Many Hoodooers incorporate sacred texts into their practice, especially the *Book of Psalms* or the *Book of Job*.

Independent Eclectic

Most modern witches are not affiliated with any one specific tradition. Most witches incorporate whatever works for them or complements their own spiritual beliefs. Urban witches, in particular, may have many influences that are then integrated and incorporated in independent and eclectic ways. No one category may be sufficient to identify their practice; hence they are independent and eclectic.

Jewitchery

This informal and eclectic tradition incorporates witchcraft, magical practice, and often shamanism with Judaism or Jewish self-awareness. Emphasis is placed on individualism. A Jewitch may or may not be a religious Jew. Judaism may be understood as a tribal group rather than as religion, and so essentially a Jewitch is someone who identifies as both Jewish and as a witch.

Some Jewitches incorporate traditional Jewish folk magic or Jewish angelology into their practice. Others identify with pre-exile or pre-Second Temple Jewish traditions that may have been less monotheistic than modern Judaism. Still others identify with Canaanite traditions. Jewitches may or may not also consider themselves Jewish Pagans. Some Jewitches are Wiccan; others are not.

Kitchen Witchery

Kitchen witchery is a practice, rather than a specific spiritual or magical tradition. What distinguishes the kitchen witch from other witches is that the majority of her tools and ingredients are readily found in the home.

A kitchen witch can cast a spell using ingredients found in her kitchen cupboards. Her magical tools may or may not be indistinguishable from ordinary household tools.

The concept of kitchen witchery is ancient. For centuries, it was not safe to be an obvious witch. Low-key, discreet magical practice helped keep witchcraft—and witches—alive. Most kitchen witches are solitary practitioners who are well-versed (or learning to be well-versed) in herb lore and folk magic. Much kitchen witchery involves magical protection of the home and family. Associations with the kitchen are no accident; spells are often cast in the form of delicious meals. A kitchen witch might be conscious of stirring eggs in a clockwise (also known as sun-wise) direction, for instance, in order to draw in positive solar energy. A synonym for kitchen witch is hearth witch.

A kitchen witch also refers to a kind of doll, a household amulet in the form of a flying witch that is traditionally hung up in the kitchen to bring good luck. These kitchen witches are of Scandinavian origin and recall Swedish Easter witches. (In Sweden, witches are associated with Easter, rather than Halloween. Children dress up as witches for parades and folkloric traditions similar to American trick-or-treating. Swedish Easter witches wear the guise of old peasant women, rather than black hats and dresses.)

Non-Wiccan Witches

This term was invented in response to the now-common assumption that all modern witches are Wiccan. Non-Wiccan witches may belong to any tradition other than modern Wicca. Non-Wiccan witches may belong to any spiritual or religious tradition or none—agnostic or atheist witches are typically considered non-Wiccan. Shamanic witches who perceive spirits as unique individual beings rather than as aspects of the Lord and Lady may also identify as non-Wiccan. Those who do not subscribe to the Wiccan Rede are, by definition, non-Wiccan.

Shamanic Witchcraft

By definition, shamanic witches blend elements of shamanism into their witchcraft. Some use the term "shamanic witch" to indicate a spirit worker, but a shamanic witch may incorporate trance and shamanic soul journeying into her practice, practices not necessarily done by a spirit worker. Please see page 128 for more information about spirit working.

Traditional Witchcraft

This is a loose definition; there are many schools and kinds of Traditional Witchcraft. Essentially, traditional witches are practitioners of forms of witchcraft that pre-date modern Wicca and New Age practices. Some people use this term to refer to hereditary traditions that are exclusive to specific families. Others use the term for specifically British traditions pre-dating Gardnerian Wicca. Others consider traditional witchcraft to be a worldwide phenomenon that refers to any practitioner of folk magic.

Wicca

Although some people use the word "Wiccan" as a synonym for any kind of witch, in general, Wiccans

perceive Wicca to be a specific religion or spiritual tradition, not just magical practice, which may or may not be encouraged. By definition, Wiccans subscribe to the Wiccan Rede, which states, *Do what you will but harm none*. (*Rede* is an archaic word for "rule.") Those who do not subscribe to the rede are not Wiccan.

Wiccans worship a male and a female deity, the Lord and the Lady. (Dianic Wicca is an exception, as most Dianic Wiccans only worship the feminine divine.) Wicca has a religious calendar, as does any other religion. Festivals, known as sabbats and esbats, honor the Wheel of the Year, the cyclical turning of nature's seasons. The most famous Wiccan sabbat is Samhain, which falls on Halloween. Other Wiccan sabbats include Beltane, Imbolc, and Yule. Wicca tends to be an initiatory religion, but it is not exclusively so. There are different denominations of Wicca, with different rules and restrictions, in the same way as Protestant denominations.

Modern Wicca is based on the teachings of Gerald Gardner, but the word is also sometimes used to refer to pre-Gardnerian British witchcraft traditions, as in Rhiannon Ryall's 1989 book, *West Country Wicca: A Journal of the Old Religion*. To add to the confusion, there are also those, usually outsiders to witchcraft, who perceive the word "witch" to be derogatory, like a racial slur. They may use the word "Wiccan," perceived as less offensive, as a generic synonym for "witch" because they are trying their best to be polite.

CHAPTER 2

A Cavalcade of Witches:

The Famous, the Infamous, and the Influential

Witches come from all walks of life, espouse different philosophies, and are masters of many arts. Here is a sampling of some of the most notorious, renowned, and influential. They derive from all over the world and represent different magical traditions.

These particular witches are literally exceptional because most practitioners of the magical arts have historically plied their crafts in private. Until *very* recently, it was dangerous to do otherwise. From the vantage point of the 21st century, where civil rights, freedom of expression, and society's tolerance may be taken for granted, it can be difficult to comprehend the sheer bravery of those first witches who emerged publicly from the broom closet and boldly proclaimed "I am a witch," the opening sentence of Sybil Leek's 1968 autobiography, *Diary of a Witch*.

For centuries witches were suppressed, oppressed, and persecuted. Witches were falsely assumed to be minions of Satan. Britain's last law against witchcraft was repealed only in 1951. Before the repeal of that Witchcraft Act, it was illegal to publish books that might be construed as encouraging the practice of witchcraft. This book that you hold in your hand would not have been published. You would not have been permitted to read it.

Well into the 20th century, witches were commonly viewed with revulsion and disgust. At best, witches were considered immoral and disgraceful. Even now, there are many places where witches feel safer tucking their pentacle pendants inside their clothing rather than wearing them outside where anyone may see. Those very first pioneering public witches—this book features Gerald Gardner, Sybil Leek, Ray Buckland, Leo Martello, and Laurie Cabot but there are others, too—bravely challenged deeply-ingrained stereotypes so that witches could be discussed without hysteria and so that new generations of witches could practice in peace.

Abei no Seimei

Sorcerer supreme and subject of literally countless tales and legends, Abei no Seimei is to Japan what Merlin is to Britain. Unlike Merlin, however, there is no debate as to when or even whether Abei no Seimei lived. A historically documented person, he was born in approximately 921 AD. A brilliant and accomplished alchemist, exorcist, astrologer, and diviner, many consider Abei no Seimei to be the ultimate master of the Japanese mystical art, *Onmyo-do.*

Literally "the way of Onmyo," Onmyo-do involves the magical mastery of Earth's inherent yin and yang forces as well as the five elements. (Japanese tradition considers metal to be an element in addition to earth, air, fire, and water.) Practitioners of Onmyo-do are called *onmyoji,* which is sometimes translated as "yin-yang master."

Like Merlin, Abei no Seimei was rumored to have unusual ancestry. His mother was allegedly a fox spirit. Abei no Seimei's magical powers manifested in early childhood: he could converse with birds and see spirits. He grew up to be a court magician, serving six emperors. Although accomplished at virtually all magical arts, his specialty was removing curses.

Following his death in 1005, Abei no Seimei was enshrined in Osaka, where every September a festival is held in his honor. Other shrines dedicated to him include the Seimei-jinja Shrine in Kyoto. Abei no Seimei is the subject of the 2001 Japanese hit film, *Onmyoji,* and its follow-up, *Onmyoji II* (2003). He also appears in the anime series, *Magical Shopping Arcade Abenobashi.*

Agrippa

Henricus Cornelius Agrippa von Nettesheim or Agrippa, for short, is widely acknowledged to be among the greatest and most influential of all magicians ever. His monumental opus, *Three Books of Occult Philosophy*, is the cornerstone of Western occultism. Born on September 14, 1486 to a noble family in Cologne in what is now modern Germany, Agrippa

was a low-key, modest man who never flaunted his aristocratic credentials.

Demonstrating an insatiable desire for knowledge, Agrippa absorbed information from every source available to him— and then some! He studied theology and philosophy at university and learned from the Roma (Gypsies) with whom he traveled. He studied Hermeticism in Italy and Kabbalah with Jewish masters, publicly acknowledging them during an era when the Church suggested that Kabbalah was diabolical.

Agrippa was a magician, alchemist, astrologer, diviner, allegedly a necromancer, and master of virtually every occult art. Although periodically hired to teach at various European universities, he mainly supported his family by working as a physician, although technically he was *not* one. He was, however, a gifted, skilled, and dedicated healer. When Europe was beset by recurrent plagues and epidemics, Agrippa stayed to minister to the sick even as licensed physicians fled from contagion.

Agrippa spent much of his own life on the run, always one step ahead of witch hunters. His free thinking and sharp tongue often landed him in trouble, earning him accusations of heresy. His life was a rotating wheel of fortune: sometimes noble patrons provided generous financial support; at other times he was tossed into debtor's prison or jailed for insulting the rich and powerful.

When a young peasant girl in Metz was arrested as a witch because her mother had been condemned for that crime, Agrippa, then serving as public advocate, protested on her behalf, claiming heredity was insufficient cause for arrest. Although unable to prevent the girl from being tortured, he was able to secure her acquittal. The upshot was that he, too, was accused of witchcraft. Agrippa fled immediately to his hometown, Cologne, but the Inquisition continued to harass him. The Holy Roman Emperor Charles V accused Agrippa of heresy and sentenced him to death. With the help of friends, Agrippa escaped to France. His destination was Lyon but he became sick en route and died in Grenoble in 1535.

Agrippa is among the mighty magicians who appear on Chocolate Frog playing cards in the *Harry Potter* novels. An English edition of Agrippa's *Three Books of Occult Philosophy*, annotated by occult scholar Donald Tyson, was published in 1992.

Bardon, Franz

Born on December 1, 1909 in what is now the Czech Republic, Franz Bardon is renowned among magical adepts, especially ceremonial magicians, but is virtually unknown to the general public. Much of his career was spent behind Communism's Iron Curtain. He ran fatally afoul of the law and it was dangerous for those who knew him to speak publicly about him.

Bardon was a magical adept, a miracle healer who specialized in herbal and homeopathic cures, a diviner, and a psychic. He worked with a magic mirror but could also see the future by gazing into a cup of coffee. Bardon began manifesting tremendous psychic ability in his youth. His gifts were well-known locally. He helped police find missing people and located lost or stolen property for neighbors.

During the 1920s and 30s, Bardon worked as a stage magician in Germany while simultaneously pursuing magical studies. He may or may not have belonged to various occult lodges. In 1933, when the Nazi party ascended to power, occult organizations were shuttered and persecuted (although the Nazis did cultivate certain individual magical practitioners).

Details are hazy, but apparently an indiscretion by one of Bardon's students drew Nazi attention to both Bardon and the student. The men were arrested and tortured, allegedly to determine whether they possessed true magic powers. While being beaten, the student, unable to help himself in a moment of great stress, uttered a Kabalistic formula, instantly paralyzing his attacker. The student was shot and killed. Bardon was ordered to reveal the names of other adepts and to work for the Third Reich, but he refused. He remained imprisoned, undergoing further torture, such as surgery without anesthesia.

When the camp in which he was held was bombed by allied forces, Bardon escaped, returning home to what was then Czechoslovakia. There, he supported his family by working as a mechanic, graphologist (handwriting analyst), and naturopath. He was arrested by local police in 1949 and charged with being a charlatan. He served two months of hard labor before being released.

Bardon authored three books: *Initiation into Hermetics, The Practice of Magical Evocation*, and *The Key to the True Kabbalah*, which together comprise a coherent, cohesive magical system. Bardon also developed a reputation as a miraculous healer. He allegedly cured at least one case of multiple sclerosis as well as several cases of terminal cancer. People flocked to him, earning him attention and hostility from the local medical establishment, who perceived him as competition.

In early 1958, Bardon was arrested again, although why has never been clear: he was never formally charged, and never brought to trial. Various theories have emerged: that he may have been suspected of spying for the West (following the publication of his books, much of his clientele traveled to see him from West Germany, Austria and Switzerland); that he failed to pay taxes on alcohol purchased to craft his tinctures; or that authorities wished to conduct experiments on him.

Imprisoned in Brno on March 26, 1958, Bardon died in a prison hospital on July 10, 1958 of unexplained causes. His family was not permitted to view his corpse, which was returned for burial in a sealed coffin. Persistent rumors suggest that he did not die in 1958, but was secretly transported to the Soviet Union where his healing methods could be further studied.

Bishop, Bridget

The first person to be hanged as a witch during the Salem witch trials, Bridget Bishop was born in England between 1632 and 1637. At the age of approximately twenty, Bridget moved to Salem, Massachusetts with her first husband. On April 18, 1692, she was arrested on charges of witchcraft. During her two-day trial, she consistently denied all charges, protesting her innocence literally up until her last breath. Had she admitted guilt, she would only have been imprisoned and her life would have been spared.

It is now generally acknowledged that most, if not all, of the "Salem witches" were not really witches. Bridget Bishop may have been an exception. Some modern scholars believe that, if not actually a witch, she was well-versed in traditional English folk magic. It is likely that many Puritans sincerely believed her to be a witch. Rumors had swirled about her for years.

Bridget was a tempestuous, sharp-tongued, unconventional, flamboyant, and independent woman living in a rigid, fundamentalist society. She was *not* submissive or obedient. Bridget married three times; her first two husbands died. She fought publicly with her husbands, behavior that Puritans scorned and detested. In 1666, she married Thomas Oliver, a prominent local businessman. After one particularly violent fight, Bridget and Thomas were gagged, bound back-to-back, and forced to stand in the town square. After his death in 1679, Thomas's children from an earlier marriage accused Bridget of bewitching him, although this may have been a plan to obtain property. Bridget was brought to trial, but was acquitted for lack of evidence. Her third husband, Edward Bishop, helped found the Beverly Church, of which Bridget remained a member in good standing until her death.

Bridget entertained guests in her home late at night. One or more taverns were associated with the

Bishop family, although it is now unclear whether Bridget or her step-daughter-in-law, Sarah Bishop, was the actual proprietress. (Sarah Bishop and her husband were also accused and arrested as witches, but they escaped from jail and remained in hiding until the witch hysteria subsided.) Bridget served and drank hard cider, an alcoholic beverage, and played games like checkers and shovel board. By Puritan standards, she dressed provocatively, and is described as wearing a black cape, black hat, and "a red paragon bodice bordered and looped with different colors." Her mode of dress was used as evidence against her at her 1692 trial. The fact that her business and lands thrived while those of other locals did not was also considered evidence of witchcraft.

Several men, including her sister's husband, testified against Bridget, as did the young girls at the center of the Salem witch accusations. Poppets made from rags and pierced with hogs' bristles were allegedly found hidden in a house she once owned. The poppets were not produced in court, and there is no proof that they existed or were made by Bridget; however, these little dolls were considered incontrovertible evidence against her.

Bridget Bishop was executed on June 10, 1692. On her way to Gallows Hill, a board spontaneously fell from a building as she passed, further cementing her accusers' conviction that Bridget was a witch.

Bridget Bishop still haunts Salem. Her ghost has allegedly been witnessed at sites historically associated with her. She is also the subject of several trial reenactments and theatrical productions. Because of the poppets, Bridget has become associated with the use of poppets in magic spells.

Blavatsky, Helena Petrovna

Hailed as the Mother of the New Age, Helena Blavatsky was among the first to introduce Buddhism and other Eastern philosophies to the West. Many modern New Age movements, as well as theories of the lost continents of Atlantis and Lemuria, are based on her writings. She is commonly called Madame Blavatsky or known by her initials, HPB.

Born in Russia on August 12, 1831 to an aristocratic family, Helena learned Russian folk magic from household servants. As a child, local peasants considered her a witch, believing her to be in league with the Rusalka, dangerous Russian mermaid-fairies who allegedly did little Helena's bidding.

At age seventeen, Helena married a significantly older man, but the marriage lasted only three months.

Helena then left Russia to travel the world. She may have lived in Tibet for seven years. She may have studied with Kabbalists in Egypt and Voodooists in New Orleans. She is known to have worked as a bareback rider in a circus and a spirit medium in Paris.

Arriving in New York City in 1873 with only enough money to buy her passage, Helena worked in a sweatshop sewing purses and as a spirit medium. It was the heyday of modern American Spiritualism, and through Spiritualist circles, Helena met author and attorney, Henry Steel Olcott. Together they would found the Theosophical Society, an organization dedicated to universal brotherhood, emphasizing the study of ancient religions, philosophies, sciences, and spiritual traditions.

Helena ran a salon out of her apartment that was frequented by a wide variety of adepts, esotericists, and Spiritualists. She developed a reputation as a formidable witch, able to perform feats of magic. She allegedly demonstrated telepathy, clairvoyance, clairaudience, levitation, and out-of-body travel. Blavatsky could also allegedly materialize objects out of thin air. Some held her in awe; others insisted she was a fraud.

Her magnum opus, her book *Isis Unveiled*, was published in 1877 and became a bestseller. She claimed the information in the book was not derived from human sources but had been given to her by divine beings she called The Mahatmas or Ascended Masters. Fans of *Isis Unveiled* included Thomas Edison and Mohandas

Gandhi. A second book, *The Secret Doctrine*, was published in 1888. Blavatsky died on May 8, 1891. The anniversary of her death is celebrated by Theosophists and known as White Lotus Day.

Buckland, Raymond

Born in London on August 31, 1934, Raymond Buckland is a leading author and authority on witchcraft, divination, Spiritualism, ghosts, and all things occult. Buckland is the person who first introduced Gardnerian Wicca to the United States.

Of Romany descent, Buckland has dedicated himself to metaphysical study since he was twelve years old, when an uncle introduced him to Spiritualism. In the late 1950s, having read Gerald Gardner's book, *Witchcraft Today*, Buckland began corresponding first with Gardner and then with Gardner's high priestess, Lady Olwen (Monique Wilson).

Buckland immigrated to the United States in 1962, where he became Gardner's spokesman. Returning to Britain briefly in 1963, he was initiated into Gardner's witchcraft tradition by Lady Olwen. In 1973, Buckland founded his own denomination, Seax-Wica, a more open, democratically organized branch of Wicca inspired by Anglo-Saxon traditions. An extremely prolific writer, he is the author of over fifty books, both fiction and non-fiction. Among his most recent are *The Weiser*

Field Guide to Ghosts, published in 2009, and *Buckland's Book of Gypsy Magic*, published in 2010.

Cabot, Laurie

High priestess, author, educator, civil rights activist, and founder of the Cabot Tradition of Witchcraft, Laurie Cabot, born March 6, 1933, is a pioneer among witches. She was among the first to practice witchcraft openly. In 1971, she opened the very first witch store in Salem, Massachusetts. In 1977, the Governor of Massachusetts, Michael Dukakis, named Laurie Cabot the Official Witch of Salem. Cabot ran for mayor of Salem in 1987, although she eventually dropped out of the race, citing other professional commitments. She is the founder of the Witches' League for Public Awareness (WLPA) and Project Witches Protection (PWP), watchdog organizations that prevent discrimination against witches and combat misconceptions and stereotypes. Her publications include *The Power of the Witch, Love Magic, The Witch in Every Woman*, and *Celebrate the Earth*.

Cagliostro,
Count Allesandro di

Alchemist, astrologer, clairvoyant, healer, and master perfume blender, Count Allesandro di Cagliostro was simultaneously a charlatan, thug, pimp, thief, con artist, counterfeiter, and forger. He remains among the most famous and influential of all magical practitioners. Centuries after his death, the name *Count Cagliostro* remains synonymous with "magician."

Of course, that really wasn't his name and he wasn't really a count; he wasn't any kind of aristocrat. His real name was Giuseppe Balsamo, and he was born poor in Palermo, Sicily on June 2, 1743. His father, a jeweler, died bankrupt just a few months after Giuseppe's birth. Raised by his widowed mother, Giuseppe grew up in Palermo's poorest, toughest slum.

As a boy, Giuseppe led a street gang and brawled with police. Yet he also displayed a brilliant intellect. Relatives contributed money for tutors, and he received an excellent education despite his predilection for landing in trouble. Giuseppe learned esoteric, intellectual, *and* criminal arts simultaneously. He spent several years as a novice monk in a monastery, learning alchemical and Hermetic secrets, but was also constantly in trouble with the law, accused of theft, thuggery, fraud, forgery, and counterfeiting. He was always on the verge of imprisonment although prominent connections kept him from jail.

Giuseppe Balsamo eventually vanished from the face of the Earth. He apparently spent the next several years traveling through Europe before resurfacing as the elegant mystic Count Cagliostro. Cagliostro's life remains mysterious. There are many gaps in the narrative. He spent time in London, Paris, and St. Petersburg. He became prominent in magical and Masonic circles, courted publicity, and developed a reputation as a wicked, dangerous man. Casanova was jealous of him.

Count Cagliostro is most famous for his role in the Affair of the Queen's Necklace. In 1784, he was arrested in Paris, accused of conspiring to steal a priceless diamond from Queen Marie Antoinette as well as of forging steamy love letters in her name (that were *not* addressed to the king!). Although Cagliostro did engage in criminal behavior, in this case, he may have been innocent. It's believed that the true conspirators may have assumed that, with his reputation, he would be the instant fall-guy. Instead, he was acquitted, but banished from France anyway.

Cagliostro was generous to the poor, operating what were essentially food kitchens out of his own pocket, long before the concept of food kitchens existed. He founded orphanages and maternity hospitals. He was a Robin Hood figure who ran free clinics for the poor while stealing from the rich.

One cannot overemphasize what a brilliant occultist he was. Simultaneously a con artist *and* the real thing, Cagliostro knew virtually all aspects of magic. He was a ceremonial magician and a folk magician, concocting love potions for a price. A pioneering Freemason, Cagliostro founded the tradition of Egyptian Freemasonry whose lodges accepted both women and men as members. (In the 21st century, acceptance of women remains controversial in some Masonic lodges.)

Cagliostro was eventually persuaded by his wife Serafina to return to their native Italy, even though Freemasonry had been condemned by the Roman Catholic Church and the Inquisition was hunting masons as if they were witches. Upon their return, possibly in an attempt to end their marriage and his total control over her, Serafina denounced Cagliostro to the Inquisition. Pope Pius VI personally issued the search warrant and ordered Cagliostro seized. Arrested on September 27, 1789, Cagliostro was interrogated forty-five times over fifteen months with the pope himself sometimes in attendance. Sentenced to life imprisonment in the Fortress of San Leo, considered Europe's most impenetrable fortress, he died on August 6, 1795. His body was tossed into an unmarked grave.

Cagliostro was the inspiration for the magician Sarastro in Mozart's opera, *The Magic Flute*. Characters based on him to greater or lesser degrees appear in many novels and films. Actors who have portrayed Cagliostro include Orson Welles and Christopher Walken.

Catherine de Medici

Born April 13, 1519, Catherine di Medici, the Italian wife of French King Henri II, became Regent of France after Henri's death, just as Nostradamus predicted she would. Catherine made no secret of her interest in magic and metaphysics. Many considered her a witch, although she was too powerful to ever be accused directly. Catherine allegedly practiced mirror divination, and may be the prototype for the evil queen mirror-gazer in the fairy tale, Snow White.

Catherine introduced astrology to the French court and surrounded herself with astrologers, magicians, and seers, including Nostradamus and Italian astrologers Cosimo Rugieri and Luc Gauric. Rugieri, Catherine's personal astrologer, made money on the side by crafting wax images that allegedly enabled those who bought them to seduce or kill a targeted person. Catherine died on January 5, 1589.

Cochrane, Robert

Born on January 26, 1931, Robert Cochrane, a graphic
artist and blacksmith, is most renowned as a philosopher, poet, and pioneering English witch. His birth
name was Roy Bowers. Cochrane founded his coven,
The Clan of Tubal Cain, at approximately the same
time that Gerald Gardner began his own first coven in
the early 1950s. Unlike Gardner, Cochrane shunned
publicity and so was overshadowed by the more media-
friendly Gardner. (Cochrane disliked Gardner and
Gardnerian Wicca intensely.)

Cochrane incorporated shamanism, ancient Celtic
mysticism, and traditional witchcraft into his tradition, as well his interpretations of Druidry. On June 21,
1966, Midsummer's Eve, Cochrane consumed the seda-
tive/hypnotic pharmaceutical Librium and the poisonous herb belladonna, more ominously known as deadly
nightshade. Hospitalized, he died nine days later, on
July 3, without ever regaining consciousness. His death
remains controversial: some believe it was accidental,
while others perceive it as suicide or as an act of ritual
self-sacrifice, timed to coincide with the solstice.

Cochrane's teachings and philosophy remain highly
influential. His articles and correspondence were published posthumously in the books *The Roebuck in the
Thicket* and *The Robert Cochrane Letters*. According to
Cochrane, "A driving thirst for knowledge is the fore-
runner of wisdom."

Crowley, Aleister

Aleister Crowley reveled in his bad reputation and would probably be very disappointed if it was not mentioned that he was known in his time as Earth's wickedest man. Founder of the magical and spiritual tradition Thelema, Crowley claimed to be the Beast whose number is 666, as described in the apocalyptic New Testament Book of Revelation.

Crowley was born on October 12, 1875 in Warwickshire, England to a wealthy family who belonged to the most conservative branch of the Plymouth Brethren, an ultra-conservative evangelical Christian movement. Crowley's father was a preacher for the Brethren and, as a child, Aleister preached with him. His father died when he was eleven, leaving Aleister a large inheritance and total financial independence once he reached adulthood.

By the age of twelve, Aleister had abandoned conservative Christianity. In December 1896, he began the pursuit of metaphysical studies that would last for the rest of his life. Crowley was involved in virtually all facets of the magical arts. Briefly a member of the influential metaphysical organization, the Golden Dawn, Crowley did not play well with others. Whether he was expelled or quit after disputes with the Golden Dawn's leader, Samuel MacGregor Mathers, remains subject to debate.

While traveling together in Egypt, Rose Kelly, Crowley's wife, was temporarily possessed by a spirit who identified itself as Aiwass. In April 1904, Aiwass spoke through Rose Kelly's mouth and dictated *The Book of the Law* to Crowley. These spiritual revelations became the basis for Thelema and Crowley's spiritual philosophies.

A prolific writer with a sharp wit, Crowley authored dozens of books on various topics. He also conceived a tarot deck, which he named *The Book of Thoth*. Crowley wrote the accompanying book; the illustrations on the cards were created by his friend, artist and occultist Lady Frieda Harris. Crowley also collaborated with Gerald Gardner at the formational stages of Gardnerian Wicca.

Crowley died on December 1, 1947 from a combination of bronchitis and myocardial degeneration. Aleister Crowley is among the faces in the crowd on the Beatles' *Sgt. Pepper's Lonely Hearts Club Band* album cover. He was the inspiration for Somerset Maugham's 1908 novel *The Magician*, and appears in Alan Moore's comic book series, *Promethea*.

Day, Christian

In 1692, witches were hunted and executed in Salem Village—but times change. In 2010, Christian Day, a self-identified witch—or warlock, the term he prefers—was elected to serve on the board of directors of Destination Salem, the city's tourism organization. Day has been instrumental in Salem's transformation from a city haunted by its associations with witch trials to one that welcomes the modern witch community. Interest in witches has helped fuel Salem's economy, although not without controversy. Drawing upon his extensive professional marketing and advertising experience, Day is a pivotal figure in the rebirth of witch tourism.

Christian Day was born on Christmas Day 1969 in the town of Beverly, Massachusetts, which neighbors Salem. Day's family has lived in the Salem area for generations. Describing himself as the "Liberace of the witch world," he began reading cards at age seventeen, and by eighteen, he was a witch. In 2002, Day was asked by fellow Salem witch Shawn Poirier to help organize a witches' ball. The ball's success inspired the pair to create other Halloween-related events, which eventually evolved into Salem's annual Festival of the Dead. The Salem Witches' Ball is now an annual event, as is another of Day's productions, the Vampire's Ball, which was inaugurated in 2004. In 2003, Day cocreated *HauntedSalem.com*, an online visitor's guide to the Witch City. He is the host of a radio-show, *Hex*

Education, and is the proprietor of two Salem witch stores: Hex, which opened on April 2, 2008, and Omen, which opened on April 3, 2010.

Dee, Dr. John

Queen Elizabeth I trusted Dr. John Dee, her faithful astrologer and spiritual advisor, to choose her coronation date. He chose well: she ruled for forty-five years. Dr. Dee may also have served Queen Elizabeth as a spy and informer, revealing what others said about her. An alchemist, magician, and scholar, Dr. Dee was the author of seventy-nine books, although most were published posthumously. He was also a master at divination and spirit summoning.

Dee was born in London on July 13, 1527 of Welsh ancestry, the son of a servant at King Henry VIII's court. By the time he entered Cambridge University at age fifteen to study mathematics and science, he had already acquired a reputation as an occultist. This reputation caused some to view him as unsavory: he was soon asked to withdraw from

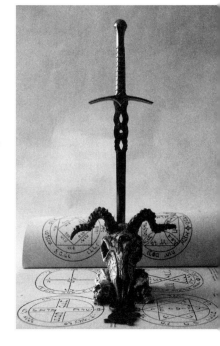

Cambridge. What first seemed to be bad luck turned out to be a golden opportunity: Dee transferred to the University of Louvain in what is now Belgium, where he was able to meet people who had personally known Agrippa, one of his heroes.

Dr. Dee originally worked for Elizabeth's predecessor, Queen Mary Tudor (a.k.a. Bloody Mary), telling her fortune daily and casting her horoscope. In the process, he became friendly with her half-sister Elizabeth, whom he would serve until her death in 1603. Allegedly Elizabeth asked Dee to cast an astrological chart that would reveal the date and nature of Mary's death. Mary found out and, outraged, threw Dr. Dee in jail on charges of witchcraft.

Imprisoned between 1553 and 1555, Dee eventually managed to talk his way out of prison, convincing authorities of his innocence. Yet his acquittal on all charges and release from prison earned him an even stronger reputation as a sorcerer. Many saw his release not as proof of his innocence but as proof of his magical power, assuming that he had glamoured his jailers into releasing him.

Dee served Elizabeth at court until his presence became a liability; Her enemies suggested that the queen spent too much time in the company of a sorcerer. Dee then spent six years traveling in central and eastern Europe, including a brief stint in Prague at the court of Emperor Rudolph II, a great devotee of the mystic arts and sponsor of many alchemists.

❧❧❧ *The Weiser Field Guide to Witches*

Dr. Dee longed to communicate with angels, but his attempts to contact them met with only inconsistent success. Dee lacked the necessary shamanic skills for spirit communications, and so he searched for partners with greater ability. The most famous of these partners was alchemist Edward Kelley. Kelley spoke with angels and Dee recorded their conversations. Together, they founded the tradition of Enochian Magic, based on these angelic communiqués.

Dr. Dee died on March 26, 1609. Prospero, the magician in Shakespeare's *The Tempest*, is believed to be based at least partially on Dr. Dee. According to author H.P. Lovecraft, Dr. Dee is responsible for translating the grimoire *The Necronomicon* into English. Dr. Dee makes an appearance in Alan Moore's comic book series, *Promethea*.

Endor, the Woman of

The mysterious Woman of Endor is the only person in the Old Testament explicitly identified as a magical practitioner. Her account appears in the First Book of Samuel 28: 7-25. Although also commonly called "The Witch of Endor," in terms of modern semantics, she is probably more accurately considered a shaman or medium. The original Hebrew phrase used to identify her is *Baalat ob*, which literally means "Mistress of the Ob."

What is an "ob," you ask? Good question—but, unfortunately, no one can answer it definitively. The word is not defined in the Bible: it may have been something so familiar that no definition was thought necessary. However, following the almost total destruction of traditional Jewish shamanism, the meaning of the word "ob" was lost. Scholars theorize that an ob was some sort of container or bottle used in divination or necromancy, perhaps a skin bag or something similar to the gourds used to house oracular spirits in some African traditions.

The first Latin translation of *Baalat ob* was "woman possessing an oracular spirit," but the King James English translation of the Bible, published during the height of Europe's witchcraze, uses the word "witch." What the Woman of Endor does is raise the dead so that she can communicate with them in a manner similar to that of a modern spirit medium.

Ironically, although the Bible is often used as an excuse to justify persecution of witches, the Bible's own account of the Woman of Endor is at worst neutral. Among his very first acts upon ascending the throne as first king of Israel, Saul forbids the practice of witchcraft, divination, and shamanism upon pain of death. However, when his own political career tanks and other approved forms of divination fail to provide the information he seeks, he orders his servants to search out a female practitioner of the old arts.

Saul's minions bring him to the woman of Endor, who is able to bring up the shade of Saul's old mentor, the prophet Samuel. Samuel is not pleased to be disturbed, and has harsh words for Saul: not only will he lose the upcoming battle with the Philistines but, within twenty-four hours, Saul and his sons will also be dead.

The Woman of Endor is not a fraud: she is genuinely able to communicate with Samuel. The information she delivers is soon demonstrated to be accurate. Significantly, she is portrayed as a woman of the community, not as a stranger. She is not depicted as a wicked witch, but as a kind woman who, having delivered unwanted news, proceeds to comfort the grieving king, urging him to eat in best Jewish mother tradition. She personally provides one of her own calves to feed the king's entourage, even though it was this king who prevented her from plying her trade openly, presumably hurting her income.

Fortune, Dion

Dion Fortune is the *nom de plume* and magical name of Violet Mary Firth, a British occultist and author whose works continue to exert influence over modern Wicca, witchcraft, and Neo-Paganism. She was born December 6, 1890 in Wales to a wealthy family engaged in the steel industry. The name Dion Fortune derives from the family motto: *Deo, non Fortuna* (God, not Fortune).

Exposed to mysticism at an early age, Fortune began having visions in childhood, including one of her past incarnation as a priestess in Atlantis. As she grew older, she became a powerful trance medium and psychic. She was briefly involved with Madame Blavatsky's Theosophical Society, but Fortune disliked Blavatsky's emphasis on the wisdom of the East.

Fortune was also initiated into the Society of the Golden Dawn in 1919, but left in 1927 to found the Fraternity of Inner Light. A staunch British nationalist, Fortune remained in London during the blitz of World War II, although her headquarters was bombed. Together with Gerald Gardner and other British witches, she participated in "Operation Cone of Power" on August 1, 1940, coordinating rituals in order to protect Britain and prevent the German invasion.

Fortune's orientation was intensely Western. Many of her interests lay in British Arthurian mythology, especially the Grail legends. Some consider modern

Wicca's almost exclusive emphasis on northern and western European magical and spiritual traditions to be largely due to her influence.

A prolific author, she began publishing both fiction and non-fiction in 1926. Fortune's books were written prior to the repeal of Britain's Witchcraft Act. It is thought that for legal reasons she obscured magical instructional material by presenting it as fiction, in the form of romantic novels. Her six books of esoteric, metaphysical fiction include *The Sea Priestess, The Goat Foot God,* and *The Demon Lover.* (Her final novel, *Moon Magic,* was completed after Fortune's death by a spirit medium allegedly channeling Fortune.) Her books remain extremely popular, although it must be cautioned that Fortune often expresses ethnic and racial bigotry that were considered acceptable in many circles during her lifetime. She died on January 8, 1946 of leukemia and is buried in Glastonbury's municipal cemetery.

Gardner, Gerald Brousseau

Author and scholar Gerald Brousseau Gardner is considered the father of modern Wicca. Born June 13, 1884, near Liverpool, to a wealthy, privileged family of Scottish descent, he spent much of his life traveling the globe, originally with the intent of alleviating his severe asthma. Much of his childhood was spent journeying to more conducive climates in the company of a nurse.

At age sixteen, Gardner was in Ceylon (now modern Sri Lanka), where he found employment in the tea industry. He spent time in the jungles of Borneo and entered government service in Malaya, becoming an inspector of rubber plantations and opium establishments. He served as a customs officer for a while. Eventually, Gardner became a rubber planter and made a fortune.

Wherever he traveled, Gardner studied local magical practices, archaeology, folklore, and anthropology. He became an authority on knives, especially their magical and ritual uses. His very first publication, *Keris and Other Malay Weapons* (1936), is still considered the authoritative work on Malay and Indonesian magical weapons.

After he retired in January 1936, Gardner returned to England and became involved with English witchcraft. He met the members of various covens in the

New Forest region, participating in their sabbats and rituals, and was initiated in 1938.

In 1946, Gardner met Aleister Crowley through a mutual friend, puppet master, occult scholar, and author, Arnold Crowther. In 1947, Gardner began his own coven. Influenced by the books of controversial witchcraft scholar Dr. Margaret Murray, Gardner determined to revive the "Old Religion." He began organizing a Book of Shadows, a compendium of rituals, poetry, and spells.

Britain's last law against witchcraft was repealed in 1951. Known as the Witchcraft Act of 1604, it had outlawed publications advocating the practice of magic. Before it was repealed, Gardner had sidestepped this law by publishing *High Magic's Aid* in 1949 in the form of a novel, essentially disguising magical instruction as fiction.

Following the repeal of the Witchcraft Act, Gardner published *Witchcraft Today* in 1954 and its companion work, *The Meaning of Witchcraft*, in 1959. Written for a general audience rather than specifically for occultists, these books would exert tremendous influence on the evolution of modern Wiccan spiritual and magical traditions. The media embraced Gardner as a spokesman for witches in general, rather than for his own specific traditions. Gardner died as he lived, traveling, on February 12, 1964, and is buried in Tunis.

John, Doctor

The birth name of this highly influential New Orleans
magical practitioner is unknown, but he is most commonly called Doctor John. Other names by which he
is known include Bayou John, John Bayou, Hoodoo
John, Voodoo John, John Montaigne, John Monet, John
Montanet, Jean Racine (*racine* is French for "root"),
Jean Gris-Gris, and Jean Macaque. Born a prince in
Senegal in approximately 1801, he was kidnapped by
slavers, brought to Cuba, and trained to work as a chef.
Allegedly, his master developed great affection for him,
and freed John in his will. John left Cuba and took to
sea, laboring as a ship's cook. He traveled the world,
including several trips back to Africa, and eventually
disembarked in New Orleans, where he would spend
the rest of his life. First employed as a cotton roller,
he became an overseer on the docks. Meanwhile, he
began plying what would become a very lucrative
magical trade.

Many claim that a skilled diviner can transform virtually anything into a divination tool. Dr. John practiced divination by interpreting the marks on bales of cotton. Clients, both black and white, began to flock to him. Dr. John worked as a magical practitioner in New Orleans from the 1820s to the 1880s, but was at the peak of his success and influence in the 1840s. By about 1850, he began to be eclipsed by his student and friend, Marie Laveau.

Described as a large, dark-skinned, very charismatic man, Dr. John's face displayed medicine scars (cicatrisation) believed to indicate Bambara heritage and royal status. In addition to being a diviner, Dr. John was also an expert astrologer, a gifted healer, and a crafter of powerful charms and talismans.

Dr. John evoked powerful emotions from other people. Although many loved and depended upon him, he utterly enraged others. Until near the end of his life when he was cheated out of his wealth and real estate holdings (although a magical adept, he was not a financial one), he lived like the prince that he was born to be, sometimes with a harem of up to fifteen women, white as well as black. In 19th-century Louisiana, this caused incredible controversy and outrage.

Known in his lifetime as the "Black Cagliostro," like his Sicilian counterpart, Dr. John ran food kitchens out of his own pocket, preparing gumbo and jambalaya for the poor and hungry of New Orleans. He died on August 23, 1885 of Bright's disease, a form of kidney dysfunction. The brilliant contemporary New Orleans musician Mac Rebennack renamed himself Dr. John in honor of this brilliant New Orleans magician.

Laveau, Marie

Among the most famous magical practitioners in the world, priestess, spirit medium, healer, diviner, and professional spell-caster Marie Laveau organized and formalized modern New Orleans Voodoo and fearlessly became the public face of what had largely been a secret, outlawed tradition. Proclaiming herself the Pope of Voodoo, she was a tremendously public figure in 19th-century New Orleans, refusing to linger in the shadows. Marie attended mass daily in a Roman Catholic Church and tended the sick during yellow fever epidemics. Notorious in her own lifetime, Marie was credited with many magical feats, including saving clients from disasters. Her specialty was legal work: through her efforts, clients and members of their families were released from prison and rescued from dire straits.

Marie's personal life remains mysterious. Her birth year is generally considered to be 1801, but it may have been earlier. Of African, European, and Native American ancestry, she was born into a Louisiana family reputedly well-versed in hoodoo and Voodoo. She was a "free person of color," a legal classification unique to French colonies, as French law distinguished between enslaved and free people of African ancestry. She was a politically conscious person who secretly helped redeem slaves and worked with the Underground Railroad to speed the endangered into safer territory.

Marie worked as a hairdresser and studied with occult practitioner Dr. John, who served as her mentor and worked closely with her. By about 1850, she was recognized as the leader of the New Orleans Voodoo community. Marie presided over annual St. John's Eve rituals at Lake Pontchartrain, where she danced with her snake, the Grand Zombi. (Not "zombi" as in the brain-eating, living dead, but a corruption of the name "Simbi," the magician snake spirit.) She became a famous celebrity. By the 1870s, thousands of spectators, white as well as black, flocked to see Marie's rituals on St. John's Eve. (St. John's Eve coincides with Midsummer's Eve, a night historically associated with witches' revelry and ritual.)

According to a famous legend, when Marie was elderly, she entered the lake, submerged, only to reemerge appearing decades younger, in the manner of a snake, rejuvenated after shedding its skin. Some interpret this as proof of her magic powers. Others claim that this was how she secretly and seamlessly retired; passing her clientele to her look-alike daughter who then assumed her mother's identity. In other words, one woman entered the water but another emerged. Both women were named Marie and used the last name

Glapion (name of the husband of one and the father of the other).

Although some believe Marie achieved immortality and roams the French Quarter still, others think she died on June 15, 1881 and that it's her ghost haunting the Quarter. In death, Marie has achieved the status of a spirit or saint. Her grave in New Orleans' oldest cemetery, St. Louis Cemetery Number One, is visited by thousands annually who come to pay tribute or beg for favors, which she reputedly delivers. In recent years, Laveau has also taken her place among the *lwa*, the pantheon of ancestral spirits of Voodoo and Vodou. Devotees consider her to be one of the Ezili family of beautiful, powerful female spirits, many of whom are closely associated with water and snakes.

Marie Laveau's celebrity status continues to extend today. Several songs in various musical genres pay tribute to her, including "Marie Laveau," the title of a 1974 song by country singer Bobby Bare. The lyrics, by poet Shel Silverstein, describe Laveau as a "lovely witch." That song has little to do with the historic Marie—the woman it describes might be any swamp witch—but it hit number one on the US country charts and its popularity furthered Marie's reputation. A more recent song, Dr. John's "Marie Laveau, Voodoo Queen," which calls her a "conjure lady," more accurately recalls her history. Marie is also the subject of novels and biographies. Dolls are crafted in her image for spiritual use and as tourist souvenirs.

Leek, Sybil

Among the first to emerge from the broom closet, publicly revealing her identity as a witch, Sybil Leek was an accomplished astrologer, fortune-teller, author, lecturer, ghost hunter, and a popular television and radio personality.

Born in what she described as a "witch-ridden" part of Staffordshire, England, near the crossroads of three rivers, Leek's birthday was February 22, but some controversy exists as to her age. Leek claimed 1922 as her natal year, but printed cards given to mourners at her 1982 memorial service gave the year 1917 instead.

Sybil was a hereditary witch from a family steeped in magic and metaphysics. On her paternal side, she claimed descent from Russian occultists affiliated with Russia's royal court. Her mother and aunt were both psychics. Her grandmother, a hedge witch and astrologer, prepared charts for such friends and house guests as Lawrence of Arabia and author Thomas Hardy.

Sybil grew up in England's New Forest region, an area with historic associations with witchcraft. Mainly home-schooled until age eleven, she never had more than a few years of conventional education, but beginning in childhood, Sybil studied witchcraft, occultism, astrology, Kabbalah, and the Bible, as well as Eastern religions, philosophies, and mystical traditions.

Aleister Crowley was a Leek family friend and predicted great things for Sybil. Another family friend,

H. G. Wells, author of *War of the Worlds*, took little Sybil to see her first eclipse. Her grandmother taught Sybil astrology by baking cookies, decorating them with astrological sigils, and asking little Sybil to put them in order or explain their significance before being permitted to eat them. Sybil herself would eventually establish what is described as the world's first astrological management consulting service.

During World War II, Sybil was a military nurse, serving for a while at the military hospital in Anzio Beach. After the war, she began to ply her trade as an astrologer. Among the clients described in her writings were the future King Hussein of Jordan, Egypt's King Farouk, and the man who deposed him, Gamal Abdel Nasser. In the 1950s, following the repeal of England's last law against witchcraft, Sybil began living openly and publicly as a witch. She published a series of articles and was interviewed by the BBC, resulting in much media attention.

For years, Sybil ran an antique store in Burley, Hampshire. As she began to attract notoriety, she was pursued by reporters and the village was besieged by tourists. When her landlord declined to renew her lease, she took this as a sign to leave England and travel to the United States. Her original intent was merely to promote a book, but she fell in love with America and elected to stay permanently, emerging as perhaps the first witch celebrity. She gave many interviews, and appeared on the Johnny Carson and Merv Griffin television talk shows. The author of over sixty books, her autobiography, *Diary of a Witch*, was published in 1969. By the time she died on October 26, 1982 in Melbourne, Florida, Sybil Leek was a millionaire.

∼⌒∘ Levi, Eliphas ∘⌒∼

Eliphas Levi is the magical name adopted by Alphonse Louis Constant, a Paris cobbler's son, born in approximately 1810. This famous occultist continues to exert tremendous influence over contemporary metaphysical practices. He was a powerful influence on the Golden Dawn, on Ceremonial Magic in general, and especially on Aleister Crowley, who, born on the very day Levi died, believed himself to be Levi's reincarnation.

Levi, then known as Alphonse Constant, was educated at Roman Catholic schools and at the seminary of Saint Sulpice, famous for its role in Dan Brown's best-selling novel, *The Da Vinci Code*. Ordained as a deacon in 1835, his church career was brief. He was expelled from Saint Sulpice, although there is debate as to why. (His occult studies may have landed him in trouble; he may have been perceived as sacrilegious; he may have had trouble with the requirements for celibacy demanded by the priesthood.)

Even before leaving Saint Sulpice, Levi had begun intensive occult studies, especially the works of Agrippa and advanced Kabbalah. He began using the Hebrew name Eliphas Levi (Levi means "priest"). His first book, *The Dogma and Ritual of High Magic*, published in 1861, connects tarot cards with Kabbalah and the twenty-two letters of the Hebrew alphabet. His other books include *The History of Magic*, *The Key of the Grand Mysteries*, and *Fables and Symbols*. According to Levi, successful magic has four requirements: knowledge, daring, will, and silence.

Levi committed his life to metaphysical study and practice, sometimes at great financial sacrifice. At one point, he was destitute and virtually homeless. Eventually, Adolphe Desbarolles, a successful palm reader, came to his aid, arranging for him to live in a lovely Parisian home. Levi began attracting students and taught various occult arts until he died on October 12, 1875.

Libuse

According to a Czech legend, witches once governed the Czech nation. Krok, the first chief of the Czechs, founded an academy of spiritual, magical, and mystical wisdom. He had three talented daughters: Kazi, an herbalist, master healer, and spell-caster; Teta, a priestess and diviner; and the youngest, Libuse, a psychic visionary and witch.

Krok died in 690 AD and was succeeded as tribal leader by Libuse (pronounced *lee-bush-uh*). In a trance, Libuse prophesied the rise of the city of Prague, advising the Czechs about where to build the city and its castle. She also located minerals underground. She foresaw wealth deriving from those minerals, and trouble deriving from that wealth.

Among her functions as tribal leader, Libuse served as a judge. After she decided a land dispute between two neighbors, the man who lost challenged her authority, complaining that only Czech men were ruled by women—whereas other nations had male rulers. Libuse put his complaint to popular vote. Either she would remain leader or she would marry and her husband would assume her position. Although she left it to the people to decide, Libuse warned that if the second option was chosen, the Czechs would ultimately regret their decision, prophesying that a male leader would confiscate their children and livestock.

Her warning was ignored. Those desiring a male ruler won the vote. Setting her white horse free, Libuse told people to follow it. The horse led them to a man plowing a field. Przemysl, the ploughman, married Libuse and took over day-to-day rule of the nation, marking the end of witch-rule and the beginning of the Przemyslid Dynasty, which ruled Czech lands from the 9th century until 1306.

Libuse is popularly considered the mother of the Czech nation. She is the inspiration for many works of art, including paintings and statues. The ruins of a 14th-century watchtower in the Vysehrad section of Prague are known as Libuse's Baths.

Martello, Dr. Leo

Among the first public witches in America, Leo Martello was born in Dudley, Massachusetts on September 26, 1931. He developed an interest in divination during his teens, studying tarot, palmistry, and graphology (handwriting analysis). At age eighteen, Leo moved to New York City to attend Hunter College and began his transition from Roman Catholicism to traditional pre-Christian Italian beliefs. In 1950, he founded the American Hypnotism Academy in New York.

Leo's grandmother had been a *strega maga* (traditional Italian witch) in Sicily. In 1951, Leo was initiated into her coven and tradition. In 1955, Leo Martello was awarded a Doctorate of Divinity degree from the National Congress of Spiritual Consultants.

His witchcraft studies continued. Martello spent a year in Morocco, studying traditional magical practices, and was initiated into Gardnerian, Alexandrian, and Traditionalist Wicca. His first book, *Weird Ways of Witchcraft*, was published in 1969.

On Halloween, 1970, Martello sponsored the first public magic circle in New York's Central Park (a "witch-in" during the era of the love-in, bed-in, and peace-in). Originally denied a permit, Martello went to the New York Civil Liberties Union and threatened a lawsuit because of discrimination. Suddenly a permit was forthcoming.

Martello was instrumental in establishing three organizations: The Witches' Liberation Movement and WICA (Witches International Craft Association) as well as the Witches' Anti-Defamation League. He drafted a Witch Manifesto in which, among other demands, he requested a National Witches' Day Parade (similar to Thanksgiving or Memorial Day parades). He also proposed a multi-million-dollar lawsuit against the Vatican for its participation in and sponsorship of the Burning Times, with reparations to be paid to descendants of the executed. Leo Martello died on June 29, 2000.

Merlin

Until the emergence of *Harry Potter*, Merlin may have been the most famous magician in the world—his very name a synonym for wizardry. Merlin is the star of countless works of fiction, most notably T. H. White's *The Once and Future King* and *The Book of Merlyn*.

It is unclear if and when Merlin ever lived. His origins are shrouded in those proverbial mists of time. It is possible that he was originally a deity—one Welsh medieval manuscript suggests that Britain was once named *Clas Myrddin* (Merlin's Enclosure) in his honor. He may also be a deified ancestor. Although usually described as of Welsh origin, Merlin is also claimed by Brittany, Scotland, and Ireland.

Merlin was not just a wizard; he was also a poet, prophet, and teacher. According to some legends, he tutored Morgan Le Fey. According to others, she tutored him. The most famous legends of Merlin recount his relationship with Britain's King Arthur.

Merlin magically orchestrated the meeting between Arthur's parents that resulted in Arthur's conception. He then served as Arthur's tutor and supervised his upbringing until Arthur was ready to ascend the throne. Even then, Merlin continued to advise and protect him. Coincidentally or not, it is when Merlin vanishes from the Arthurian saga that the dreams of Camelot and the Round Table begin to deteriorate. No other advisor ever replaces Merlin.

There are various accounts of what befell Merlin. Most involve a female magician under whose spell he falls, although the identity of his femme fatale varies. Merlin may sleep, trapped in a crystal cave. He may be magically bound in some alternate dimension.

Alternatively, some legends suggest his departure was voluntary. One legend suggests that he transformed himself into an oak in despair over a romantic rejection; another that he abandoned Britain following the adoption of Christianity, traveling with a company of bards to Bardsey Island off the coast of North Wales, taking with him Britain's legendary Thirteen Treasures. Local Bardsey lore suggests that Merlin is buried in a cave on the island. (Other legends suggest that King Arthur is buried there, too.)

There are *countless* legends featuring Merlin, many having nothing to do with Arthur. Some legends are contradictory; they may not all be about the same person. In most versions, Merlin's mother is a princess. His father is a mystery.

Some tales describe Merlin's father as a wild man of the woods; others suggest that he was a demon. Identifying Merlin as demon-spawn may be a Christian attempt to vilify a Pagan magician, or it may be a vestige of even older myths in which Merlin is a demigod, the magical child of a spirit father and a mortal mother.

Merlin also once had strong popular associations with Stonehenge, although these are now discounted by historians and archaeologists. It has been suggested that Merlin was worshipped at Stonehenge, or even that he was responsible for its construction.

Moses

Occult scholar Henri Gamache described Moses as "the great Voodoo man of the Bible." The biblical prophet is considered to be among the most powerful magicians of all time. In the first century, Pliny the Elder, writing about Jewish magicians, described Moses as the greatest of them. The New Testament's Books of Acts 7:22 states that "Moses was educated in all the learning of the Egyptians and he was a man of power in words and deeds." Magic was the "learning" with which ancient Egypt was most closely associated at the time the Book of Acts was written.

Raised in the Egyptian palace, Moses was allegedly schooled by royal priests who taught him advanced ritual magic. He was also familiar with other forms of magic: his mother and sister Miriam were both midwives, a profession closely associated with Jewish folk magic. Moses' father-in-law, Jethro, was a Midianite shaman. (After losing his temper and killing an Egyptian overseer who was mistreating a Hebrew slave, Moses fled into the deserts of Midian, where he lived for forty years before returning to Egypt to free the Israelites. Midian may be located in Israel's Negev desert, in Saudi Arabia, or near the Gulf of Aqaba.) Moses' wife, Zipporah, Jethro's eldest daughter, is described as one of seven sisters. "Seven sisters" is a phrase with powerful magical resonance because of its association with the Pleiades and star magic. Among the legends surrounding Moses is that he was cast into a pit for ten years where he was secretly tended and cared for by Zipporah. This story may be interpreted as describing a shamanic incubation ritual.

Moses' rescue of the Hebrew slaves was accomplished via what at least appear to be feats of magic, as, for instance, when his staff transforms into a snake and back again. When the Israelites lack water while wandering in the desert, Moses uses this same staff, albeit against God's direction, to strike a rock from which drinking water then gushes. Some consider Moses to be a water witcher.

Jewish legend suggests that when Moses was given the Ten Commandments and Torah (also known as the Five Books of Moses) on Mount Sinai, he was also given additional metaphysical and magical information not intended for common knowledge. This secret knowledge was passed down orally from magician to magician, beginning with Moses. Some of this secret lore allegedly found its way into grimoires, books of magic, especially those attributed to King Solomon, who shared a direct magical lineage with Moses. Several grimoires are attributed to Moses, too, including *The Sword of Moses, The Sixth and Seventh Books of Moses*, and *The Mystery of the Long Lost 8th, 9th and 10th Books of Moses*.

Moses is sometimes identified as Hermes Trismegistus, Father of Alchemy. Other traditions identify him with the Vodou snake spirit Simbi, who also has powerful associations with snakes, magic, and water.

Norton, Rosaleen

A devoted acolyte of the Greek deity Pan, Rosaleen Norton was a visionary artist, mystic, occultist, and witch who served as High Priestess of an Australian coven. Until recently, she was little known outside

Australia, mainly because her paintings, inspired by magical and Pagan themes, were deemed obscene, legally suppressed and rarely seen.

Rosaleen, known to friends as Roie, was born on October 2, 1917 in Dunedin, New Zealand, but moved with her family to Sydney, Australia in 1925. Beginning in early childhood, she manifested an interest in the occult, simultaneously demonstrating great creative talent. She drew passionate, mystical fantasies and wrote macabre stories. She found employment, in young adulthood, as an illustrator for a newspaper, but her work was considered too risqué and she was let go from her job.

Rosaleen continued to explore her dreams and visions via her art. She utilized techniques including self-hypnosis, trance, and automatic drawing, and her themes included ancient deities, rituals, and sex. However, as it was a conservative era in Australia, there was little tolerance for Roie's sexually explicit art and Pagan visions. In 1949, the first major exhibition of her work was held at the Rowden-White Gallery at Melbourne University. Within days of the opening, police raided the gallery, seizing four of the exhibited paintings and proclaiming them criminally obscene.

Charges were eventually dropped after various academics appeared in court to defend Roie's depictions of pantheism, but Roie's life was transformed. Overnight she became a notorious figure of scandal. The tabloid press dubbed her the "Witch of King's Cross," Sydney's red light district and bohemian center and the site of her apartment home. Rosaleen thrived in King's

Cross—local cafés displayed her murals. She became a celebrity and media favorite but the press also hounded her, accusing her of conducting orgies and black masses. Her devotion to Pan, the horned goat-footed god, was misrepresented as Satanism.

In 1952, *The Art of Rosaleen Norton*, a leather-bound, 500-copy limited edition book of her art accompanied by poetry written by her lover, Australian poet Gavin Greenlees, was published by Walter Glover. It was quickly deemed criminally obscene because it included depictions of pubic hair and "phallic appendages." The publisher, charged with indecency and producing an obscene publication, was found guilty. The books could only be distributed if some sexually explicit images, dubbed pornographic, were blacked out. United States Customs burned imported copies of the book. In 1957, Walter Glover, the publisher, was declared bankrupt and copyrights assigned to him were taken over by Australia's Official Receiver in Bankruptcy. They were finally returned to him in 1981, and a new edition of the book with all images intact was published in 1982, years after Rosaleen's death on December 5, 1979 of colon cancer.

Pleasant, Mary Ellen

The early life of Mary Ellen Pleasant is steeped in mystery. She may have been born a slave on an Augusta, Georgia plantation; other sources suggest that she was born in Philadelphia. Her birthday was August 19 in approximately 1814, but the precise year remains unknown. She claimed to be the daughter of an enslaved Voodoo priestess born in Haiti and the youngest son of the governor of Virginia.

By the 1820s, Mary Ellen Pleasant was living with and working for a Quaker family in Nantucket, Massachusetts who introduced her to abolitionism. Later, she married James Smith. Both Smith and Pleasant were fair-skinned people of mixed race who were able to pass for white. They took advantage of this in order to become actively involved in the Underground Railroad, rescuing the enslaved and bringing them to freedom and safety. In this capacity, Mary Ellen worked closely with Marie Laveau, with whom she also studied Voodoo.

Mary Ellen's husband left her a fortune when he died. She helped finance her friend John Brown's raid on Harper's Ferry. Her work rescuing slaves earned her the enmity of slavers, who put a price on her head. She escaped to San Francisco in 1852. While en route, she met Thomas Bell, the director of the Bank of California, with whom she would have a thirty-year relationship.

In San Francisco, Mary Ellen emerged as a philanthropist and entrepreneur. She ran restaurants and a boarding house, and allegedly a bordello—although this may be an attempt at defamation. She evoked powerful reactions from people, as she still does. People consider Mary Ellen Pleasant a heroine *or* a wicked, scandalous woman.

Her reputation as a Voodooist accompanied her to California, and while some perceived her as a guardian angel, others were genuinely terrified of her. The headline of an article about Pleasant in the July 9, 1899 Sunday *San Francisco Chronicle* proclaimed her the "Queen of the Voodoos." A writer described her as the "witch woman of the West." Mary Ellen Pleasant is also known as the Mother of Civil Rights in California. Long before Rosa Parks refused to give up her seat to a white man on a Montgomery, Alabama bus, Mary Ellen Pleasant sued a San Francisco streetcar company for denying service to African-Americans—and won!

Her death on January 4, 1904 did not halt the controversy surrounding her, nor apparently has she left San Francisco. Some perceive that, having died, she has evolved into a powerful spirit capable of granting wishes. Others consider her a creepy ghost. Mary Ellen Pleasant is now a fixture of San Francisco paranormal tours. She allegedly haunts the corner of Bush and Octavia streets, where her mansion, dubbed the "House of Mystery" by the tabloid press, once stood. Crows,

Mary Ellen's messenger birds, are said to signal her presence. Legend says that if you make a polite request at this corner *and* if she is in a good mood, Mary Ellen will grant your wish.

Randolph, Paschal Beverly

Perhaps the most influential unsung hero of the magical arts, Paschal Beverly Randolph was a Spiritualist, Rosicrucian, ceremonial magician, hoodoo doctor, prolific author, and occult scholar. Considered the foremost exponent of magic mirrors, he founded several metaphysical societies, including the Hermetic Brotherhood of Luxor and the Brotherhood of Eulis. Among the most influential occultists, his theories influenced Helena Blavatsky, Aleister Crowley, and many others.

Randolph was born on October 8, 1825 in New York City's brutal, crime-ridden Five Points slum, the setting for Martin Scorsese's 2002 film, *Gangs of New York*. He identified his father as a member of Virginia's prominent Randolph family. His mother, Flora, was of African descent. Randolph described his mother as psychically gifted, and he believed that he inherited his gifts from her.

By 1853, he was listed in the New York City directory as *Dr. Paschal Beverly Randolph, clairvoyant physician and psycho-phrenologist.* (Phrenology, which was very popular in the 19th century, suggests that personality traits and possibly destiny may be determined by studying the shape of the skull; it is essentially the equivalent of palm reading using the head.)

A dedicated student of the mystical arts, he was a gifted trance medium, channeling Benjamin Franklin, Napoleon, and his mother, among other spirits. An extremely handsome, articulate, and charismatic man, he was a popular favorite on the lecture circuit. Randolph studied with Voodooists in New Orleans and with dervishes in Turkey. He traveled extensively through Europe, the Middle East, and North Africa, becoming proficient in several languages including Arabic and Turkish. He studied with occultists of many traditions. In Paris he may have met Helena Blavatsky and Eliphas Levi, who may or may not have initiated him into societies to which Levi belonged.

Returning to the United States, Randolph became a publisher and entrepreneur as well as the foremost scholar and theorist of sex magic. He taught that human vitality is dependent upon *mutual* sexual fulfillment. He considered the moment of simultaneous orgasm to be the point of maximum magic power: that the vital energy that flows during what he considered "correct sexual intercourse" supports clairvoyance, psychic ability, and mediumship, and ultimately links the human soul with the celestial spheres.

In order to achieve this, Randolph taught, men and women must locate their soul mates. Randolph's life was largely dedicated to finding that soul mate. His own love life was stormy. He married at least three times. It is theorized that the seeds of Crowley's quest for his own Scarlet Woman derive at least partially from Randolph's teachings.

Near the end of his life, Randolph was consumed by bitterness. He had suffered severe financial losses and was perhaps drinking too much. He felt intense resentment that despite his many accomplishments, as a black man, he was not given the respect owed to him by other occultists, which he blamed—with much justification—on the prevalence of racism. On July 29, 1875, Paschal Beverly Randolph committed suicide in Toledo, Ohio by shooting himself with a pistol.

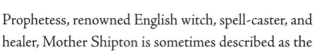

Shipton, Mother

Prophetess, renowned English witch, spell-caster, and healer, Mother Shipton is sometimes described as the English Nostradamus. Like Nostradamus, her proph-

esies appear in rhyming verse. Since 1641, over fifty versions have been published.

Details of Mother Shipton's life are hazy; various dates are suggested for both her birth and death. Her maiden name seems to have been Ursula Southeil or

Sontheil. (The name "Shipton" derives from her 1512 marriage to Tony Shipton.) The most popular legend of her birth suggests that she was born in a cave in 1488 in Knaresborough, Yorkshire. A well reputedly possessing mystical healing powers is located nearby.

Ursula's unmarried, teenage mother, Agatha, was rumored to be a witch with the power to heal, raise storms, and foretell the future. Ursula's father is unknown. Local people believed that he was the devil. Ursula was apparently orphaned at birth, her mother dying in childbirth. (Another version of Mother Shipton's life story suggests that Agatha entered a convent, abandoning Ursula when she was two.)

Raised by a local woman, Ursula's own reputation as a witch began during childhood. (The fact that neighbors considered her to be devil spawn did not help her reputation.) Little Ursula allegedly possessed powers of telekinesis, and was not averse to using them against those who weren't kind to her. Many were unkind: not only because she was associated with witchcraft and the devil, but also because Ursula is described as having been "ugly" or "deformed." (There are various theories as to possibly congenital deformities.) She cast spells over those who mocked her, aggressively defending herself with magic.

Although feared, Mother Shipton was also very much in demand because of the proven accuracy of her prophesies. Crowds, including some extremely prominent people, flocked to her for consultation. She foretold the invasion and the defeat of the Spanish Armada in 1588 and the Great Fire of London in 1666. Mother Shipton died in 1561. Her cave and the nearby well in Knaresborough can still be visited and are now tourist attractions.

Spare, Austin Osman

English artist and magician Austin Osman Spare is described as the father of Chaos Magic. The only son of a London policeman, Spare's birth date is usually given as December 31, 1886. But in true mystical, liminal fashion, Spare claimed he did not know on which side of midnight he was born—whether on the last day of 1886 or the first of 1887. (Another legend suggests that he was born at the stroke of midnight.)

Spare demonstrated a talent for art at a young age. An excellent draftsman, he studied stained glass design and in 1904 won a scholarship to the Royal College of Art. His first book was published in 1905. Initiated into witchcraft in his youth, Spare worked with automatic drawing, automatic writing, and sigils. A skilled diviner, he was able to conjure spirits. Spare met Aleister Crowley in approximately 1907, and the two began corresponding. Spare was briefly a member of the Golden Dawn.

In 1913, Spare published the *Book of Pleasure*, a magical work that includes instructions for what he called his process of sigilization. He then served in Egypt during World War I. Returning to London after a brief period of sociability and popularity, Spare essentially exiled himself to his home so that he could devote himself completely to the development of his art and magic, which for him were totally interconnected. In the late 1940s, he emerged from this seclusion to become involved with other British occultists. Spare died on May 15, 1956.

Tamamo-no-mae

A gorgeous courtesan and Tantric adept in 12th-century Japan, Tamamo-no-mae's brilliance and broad education belied her youthful looks. Although every year she became more erudite, she never seemed to age. Tamamo was not only beautiful, wise, and accomplished, but she was also kind and pleasant, and so became a great favorite at court, where she

was known as the Jewel Maiden or the Jewel without Flaw.

Emperor Konoe (1139–1155) favored her above all others and spent all his time with her. Eventually he fell mysteriously ill. All attempts to heal him failed. Finally a court magician blamed his condition on Tamamo, revealing her to be a fox witch disguised as a beautiful woman, who was magically draining the emperor of all his vital energy.

Tamamo fled from court, allegedly in the form of a nine-tailed golden fox. The emperor's finest hunters were ordered to find and kill her. She eluded them until one night she appeared in a hunter's dreams, saying that she knew she would be trapped the next day and begging for mercy. The dream was prophetic. The hunters located her on the moor of Nasu, and showed no mercy.

Shot with an arrow, Tamamo used her last breath to magically transform into a great standing stone, *Sessho-seki* ("The Murder Stone" or "Death Stone"). Anyone who came into contact with the stone or slept beneath its shadow died, until over a century later, when a Buddhist priest appeased her anger by performing rituals for Tamamo's soul and begging her to stop killing. Allegedly the stone is now safe, although travelers are still cautioned from going near it. An annual ritual, the Nasu Fire Mountain Festival, is held at the stone each year in efforts to keep Tamamo's spirit appeased. Participants wear fox masks and costumes and engage in ecstatic dance and taiko drumming.

Tamamo-no-mae is the inspiration for Noh and kabuki plays. Her portrait was created by the great Japanese woodblock master, Tsukioka Yoshitoshi.

Valiente, Doreen

Described as the "Mother of Wicca," Doreen Valiente was an eloquent poet and author of many of Wicca's most beloved rituals, including *Charge of the Goddess* (modeled on Charles Godfrey Leland's book, *Aradia*) and *The Witches' Rune*. A modest, private woman who shunned publicity all her life, she was born in London and educated at a convent school. Her clairvoyant gifts manifested early, and she studied various occult traditions as well as Theosophy. Valiente eventually met Gerald Gardner, who initiated her into his Bricket Wood Coven in 1953.

Serving as the coven's High Priestess and working alongside Gardner, Valiente revised much of his liturgy. She labored over Gardner's Books of Shadows from 1954 to 1957, deleting contributions by Crowley, whom she found offensive, and contributing her own poetry instead (much of it modeled after Leland, whom she greatly admired). Always an independent thinker, Doreen eventually had philosophical disagreements with Gardner and left his coven to form her own. In 1964, she was initiated into Robert Cochrane's Clan of Tubal Cain, but, unhappy with Cochrane's criticisms of Gardnerian Wicca, eventually left this coven, too.

Valiente was among those who publicly opposed efforts by the British government to pass new legislation against witchcraft in the 1970s. (Legislation did not pass.) Her first book, *An ABC of Witchcraft*, was published in 1973. Doreen Valiente died on September 1, 1999.

CHAPTER 3

Tools of the Trade

Witches sometimes cast spells using only the power of
their minds or their words. Charms and incantations,
for instance, are spoken spells. All they require is that
words be articulated—aloud or silently. However, over
the centuries, certain tools have become important
components of spell-casting and witchery. Many are
familiar—brooms, wands, and cauldrons are integral
to the iconography of witches. Others, like the stang or
runes, may be less familiar to the general public.

Not all witches utilize all the following tools, but
all are closely identified with witches and witchcraft.
Candles and cards are fairly modern additions to the
witch's tool box; the stang, cauldrons, and brooms are
primeval. It must be pointed out, however, that if a
witch or practitioner uses *any* tool consistently in his
or her magical work, that tool, whatever it is, is transformed into a magical tool.

Athamé

An athamé, (pronounced *a-tham-ay* or *ath-may*) is a ritual knife. Symbols, such as runes or sigils, may be engraved or painted onto the handle. It is usually black-handled, and has a double-edged steel blade. Whether that blade is sharp or dull is irrelevant because the athamé is not intended as a cutting tool and is *never* used to draw blood.

The athamé is among the standard tools of Wicca. Although the use of ritual knives, daggers, or swords is common to many magical traditions, the name and concept of the athamé is almost exclusively Wiccan or Wiccan-influenced. Among many other uses, an *athamé* is used to cast ritual circles and direct magical energy.

Bolline

A bolline is a knife intended for use as a cutting tool in Wiccan spell-casting and rituals. It is the practical counterpart to the athamé, which is exclusively a ritual tool. A bolline traditionally has a double-edge blade and a white handle, which makes it very easy to distinguish from the traditionally black-handled athamé.

The bolline's original function was to harvest herbs. Although most modern bollines are standard knives, older ones frequently featured sickle-shaped blades. It's believed that the bolline was originally a smaller version of the sickle, among the most ancient of all tools. In addition to harvesting or chopping herbs, bollines may be used for any magical working that involves cutting, like carving candles.

Book of Shadows

A Book of Shadows is a personalized, handwritten book containing a witch's spells, rituals, and wisdom. No two will be identical. The magical book passed down from generation to generation in the Halliwell family figured so prominently in the television series *Charmed* is an example of a Book of Shadows.

The concept underlying the Book of Shadows is that for centuries, people practicing witchcraft and/or Pagan religions were persecuted, and practices had to be kept secret, for safety's sake. (The Inquisition did not distinguish between witchcraft and Pagan religions, but equated the two.) Possession of any kind of magical or Pagan text could be grounds for conviction of witchcraft. The name "Book of Shadows" refers to the necessity of keeping these books safely hidden in the shadows, rather than out in plain sight.

This concept is extremely controversial. Some believe the Book of Shadows tradition to be genuinely ancient. Others are convinced that the concept was invented by Gerald Gardner. For some people, that's irrelevant: Books of Shadows are beautiful and powerful, regardless of when the concept emerged. Still others believe that if Gardner invented the tradition, then it is inauthentic.

No ancient Books of Shadows have yet been discovered, although this in itself does not prove that the tradition is not old. When accused witches were killed, it was customary for any books they owned to be confiscated and burned. According to 17th-century Venetian Inquisition records, a woman named Laura Malpero was charged with witchcraft. When her home was searched, a copy of the banned grimoire *The Key of Solomon* was discovered along with a private, handwritten book of spells and rituals into which Laura had copied parts of that famous grimoire. Laura's book, which was destroyed, fits the definition of a Book of Shadows.

 **Brooms**

Perhaps the most famous and recognizable witches' tools, brooms may first have been invented for magical and spiritual purposes. The act of sweeping has magical significance; depending on direction, sweeping over a threshold manipulates energy in or out, inviting or repelling, summoning or banishing.

Brooms are incorporated into many magic spells. Lady Alice Kyteler of Kilkenny, Ireland, whose 1320 witchcraft trial is sometimes pinpointed as the official start of Europe's witch panic, was accused of walking Kilkenny's streets with a broom, sweeping toward the house of her son, William, and chanting,

To the house of William my son,
 Hie all the wealth of Kilkenny town.

Of course, the most famous thing witches do with brooms is ride them. Countless images of witches, archaic and modern, depict them flying through the air on their brooms. Originally, the idea of witches' flight may have been shamanic, not literal. One theory regarding the origin of brooms is that they were first used as a shamanic tool for soul-journeying or trance journeys. The witch's broom may have originated as a ritual horse, intended to be "ridden" in the context of shamanic ritual. A traditional hobby horse is essentially nothing more than a broomstick with a horse's head.

Brooms have evolved into a witch's emblem, and are displayed as a badge of pride. Those who keep their witch identity secret are described as "being in the broom closet." A popular bumper sticker proclaims, "My other car is a broomstick!" Brooms are also the sacred symbols of witch goddesses Hekate and Tlazolteotl.

Candles

Among the most popular magical tools, candles and candle burning are associated with many styles of magic. However, until the 20th century and the development of paraffin wax, candles were rare and prohibitively expensive. Beeswax and tallow candles were used instead. Magic lamps were constructed by floating cotton wicks in flame-proof containers filled with oil.

Candle magic spells can be very simple or incredibly complex. The simplest candle spell involves holding a candle in your hands while focusing intently on your goals, desires, and aspirations, and then lighting the candle. A complex candle spell might incorporate several candles. Color and style of candle might be coordinated with astrological, magical, or spiritual correspondences, and candles may have to be lit at different times or in varying orders. Individual candles might be lit at a specific moment, left to burn for a specific period of time, then snuffed out and lit again at specific intervals.

Magical candles come in all shapes, colors, and sizes. In addition to taper and pillar candles, magic candles also commonly appear in the form of cats, witches, people, crosses, skulls, and genitals. Candles may be designed to burn for seven or nine days. Herbs or crystals might also be added to the candle for varying magical purposes.

Cards

Tarot cards are the most popular magical cards, although witches also utilize standard playing cards or special oracle cards. What are commonly called "Gypsy Witch Fortune-Telling Cards" are based on a card system invented by Madame Marie Lenormand (1772–1843), a renowned French astrologer and fortune-teller, whose clients included Napoleon Bonaparte and his wife Josephine.

In addition to divination, cards are also used for spell-casting, meditation, and spiritual contemplation. Before the invention of the printing press, cards were hand-crafted; many still craft their own cards for personal magical use.

Cauldrons

Double, double toil and trouble
Fire burn and cauldron bubble

Macbeth's Weird Sisters' famous chant pays tribute to this primeval magical tool. A cauldron is an old-fashioned iron pot. It may be used

for cooking, brewing potions, or spell-casting. The word *cauldron* is related to words indicating "heat" or "to warm up," and is believed to derive from the Latin *caldarium*, a "hot bath."

Ancient spells frequently assume that you have access to a hearth or similar open fire. This is rarely the case nowadays—and cauldrons provide the safest substitute when something needs to be burned. The cauldron is the emblem of divine sorcerers, including Cerridwen, Medea, and Ogun.

Crystal Balls

A crystal ball is exactly what it sounds like: a round globe formed from crystal. Crystal balls may be clear or colored crystal. They are used for divination (scrying), for spirit summoning, and for shamanic communication with other realms. Necromantic seers, those who hope to contact the dead, often prefer smoky quartz crystal balls.

Crystal balls derive from the ancient tradition of lunar gazing: either gazing directly at the moon or into a basin of water into which the moon reflects. Crystal balls are traditionally kept covered when not in use. They are cleaned using incense smoke or by careful cleansing with magical washes, usually herbal-infused spring water or spring water to which flower essences have been added.

Dolls

Not just play things, dolls serve as magical tools, too. A doll is an image of a living being—usually a person, but dolls can take the form of animals or creatures, too.

Dolls are crafted from a wide variety of materials including porcelain, clay, vinyl, wax, wood, bone, cloth, paper, straw, and virtually anything else you can think of.

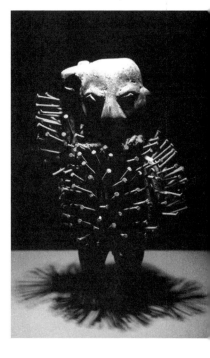

An archaic word for doll is *poppet*, which is related to *puppet*. Witches use dolls when casting fertility, healing, romantic, and protective spells as well as for malicious purposes. The most famous and notorious magical dolls are those which are intended to cause magical harm, but that may be because people enjoy discussing scandalous, dangerous, scary aspects of witchcraft and magic. Dolls are more often used for benevolent magical goals than malevolent ones.

So-called "Voodoo dolls" defame this African Diaspora spiritual tradition. The stereotypical Voodoo doll is a wax figure intended to resemble the spell-caster's target. Pins are stuck into the doll's body in order to harm the same areas on the target. In fact, this type of magic spell derives from European folk magic, not African. African dolls are rarely made from wax, and are more likely to be used for healing, protection, prosperity, and venerating spirits. Genuine Voodoo dolls—as used in Voodoo tradition—tend to be made from wood and cloth, and are crafted to resemble deities so that they may be used as altar images for purposes of veneration or spiritual petition.

Throughout east Asia, dolls serve as oracular devices. Legends describe very special dolls that are actually able to communicate prophesies. The most famous, and possibly the largest, magical doll may be the Golem of Prague. A Golem is an artificial man created from clay and brought to life by various spiritual and magical techniques. Rabbi Judah Loewe (c. 1525–1609) created a Golem to protect Prague's Jewish community from persecution, sort of a magical body guard. When it became uncontrollable, Rabbi Loewe destroyed it.

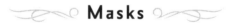 **Masks**

Masks are so closely identified with witches that an Italian synonym for "witch" is *masca*. Once upon a time in Europe, back when it was dangerous to be identified as a witch, many attended witches' balls wearing masks to protect their anonymity.

Masks resembling stereotypical witches (green face; hooked nose; big wart) are traditionally among the most popular Halloween masks, but the association of witches with masks transcends Halloween costumes. Masks are shamanic tools, portals to other realms and existences. They enable spiritual possession. Putting on a mask enables a person to enter the realm of the sacred, to become another person or another being. Masks are incorporated into spell-casting as well as magical and spiritual rituals.

Mirrors

Popular in many magical traditions, including those of ancient Egypt, Mexico, and China, as well as Western Ceremonial Magic and Italian folk magic, mirrors have many magical uses including spirit summoning, love magic, divination, and scrying. Mirrors provide protection, allegedly warding off the Evil Eye and frightening low-level demons. Wall paintings in ancient Chinese tombs show men holding mirrors facing outward so as to frighten evil spirits away from the dead. Mirrors serve as portals to other realms via scrying, and may be used in similar fashion to a crystal ball.

Modern mirrors are usually made of glass, but ancient mirrors were typically crafted from smooth metal, usually copper, which was then highly polished so as to be reflective. The ancient Etruscans, who once lived in what is now Italy, crafted exquisite magical mirrors featuring images of glamorous deities on their nonreflective sides. The Aztecs crafted magic mirrors from polished obsidian, which is black volcanic glass.

The most famous magical mirror is the one that belongs to the witch queen in the fairy tale, *Snow White and the Seven Dwarfs*. The queen gazes into her mirror and asks,

> Mirror, Mirror on the wall
> Who is the fairest of them all?

Because her mirror is no ordinary one, she receives an honest answer. In the 1937 Walt Disney animated film, *Snow White and the Seven Dwarfs*, the witch's mirror is decorated with accurate astrological sigils and appears truly magical.

Ghosts and certain types of spirits are believed to reside within mirrors. The mirror may be used as a portal to communicate with them. Dr. John Dee attempted to communicate with angels using an Aztec obsidian mirror. Spirits associated with magic mirrors include Tezcatlipoca and Lilith.

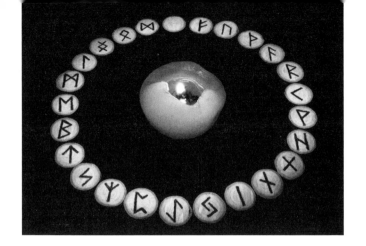

 ## Runes

A system of sacred symbols used for divination, spell-casting, and meditation, runes may also be used to contact and communicate with spirits. Although similar symbols exist or have existed in many parts of the world, modern runes are most associated with Nordic and Germanic magical and spiritual traditions.

Runes are frequently described as an alphabet, but that description only hints at their power. Each rune does have a phonetic value—they can be read and used to write words—but each also radiates a specific magical and spiritual power. Runes can be combined and manipulated so as to increase and maximize these powers. Runes provide a divination device known as "casting the runes."

Runic alphabets are known as *futharks*. The most ancient surviving full futhark is known as the Elder or Common Germanic Futhark, and consists of twenty-four runic characters in a specific order, in the same manner that an alphabet's letters are arranged in specific order. Just as there is alphabetical order, so there is runic order.

Rune sets consist of small individual pieces, each inscribed with a different rune. Runes are traditionally made from strips of bark, but small pieces of leather may also be used. Runes are also crafted from minerals, glass, and other fine materials.

The word *rune* is believed to derive from the Indo-European root word *ru*, meaning "mysterious or secret thing" and which is also sometimes used to indicate "witch." The Old German word *runa* means "whisperer" in reference to wise women or witches who sometimes whisper or murmur spells, rather than clearly articulating them. The German words *alruna* or *alraune* are cognate with *rune* and are translated as "witch." Runes are associated with Odin, who, according to myth, sacrificed himself on the World Tree for nine nights in order to acquire knowledge of the runes.

Stang

A stang is a forked wooden staff used in spell-casting and during rituals. It resembles a wooden pitchfork. The word derives from the Old Norse, but the tool itself is used in several witchcraft traditions from around the world, including Wicca. However, it is not exclusively a northern or western European ritual tool.

British tradition recommends that a stang be crafted from ash, but other traditions may recommend different types of wood.

How the stang is used depends upon the specific tradition. The stang may serve as an altar or as a shamanic portal to other realms. It may be used like a magic wand. The stang may represent the power of the crossroads. The stang is associated with ancient horned deities and is sometimes considered a masculine tool, the counterpart to the feminine broom. It is also sometimes identified with the World Tree or the cosmic axis. Its shape may mimic horns, antlers, or even arms outstretched upward.

 Wands

It's a toss-up as to whether wands or brooms are the tools most associated with witches. Wands are used to direct magical energy. A wand may also be understood as tapping into the power of trees. Different types of wood are believed to radiate different energies, and thus suit different magical purposes. A magic wand carved from applewood, for instance, is believed especially beneficial for love magic, while a wand carved from poisonous plants like yew, oleander, or hemlock enables necromancy. Faery witches may use a rose's long stem as a wand. Some practitioners use only one wand, while others collect different wands, using each for specific purposes.

Wands may be ornamented with crystals, feathers, and amulets. They may be engraved with sigils, runes, hieroglyphs, sacred names of power, or magical inscriptions. As described in the *Harry Potter* novels, wands may be hollowed out and filled with a reed or other material.

Don't have a magic wand? Substitutions are easily made: an umbrella serves as a magic wand, as does a cane, folding fan, flute, or sometimes even a finger.

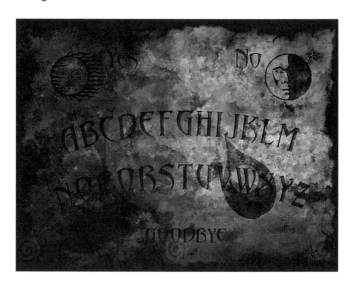

⟶ Witch Boards ⟵

Also known as spirit boards, talking boards, and Egyptian luck boards, witch boards are divination devices. Planchettes are also considered part of this magical tradition.

A witch board is a flat board marked with letters, signs, numbers, and words, for instance "yes," "no," and "maybe." The board is intended to serve as a portal to the beyond. It is a device with which to contact the inhabitants of other realms, especially those who have passed from this mortal coil over to the afterlife.

A small movable indicator, usually triangular or heart-shaped and known as a *planchette*, is used to point to the different markings on the board and thus effect communications. *Planchette* literally means "little board" in French, and was first used to describe an ancestor of the witch board, a rolling wooden board used for similar purposes and in a similar manner.

Witch boards have ancient roots as Chinese and central African divination tools. The Ouija board is the most familiar type of witch board, but other types exist. Some witch boards, like the Ouija, are mass-marketed, but others are carefully and ritually handcrafted by spiritual and magical adepts.

Witch boards may also be improvised by using a shot glass or tumbler and individual letters. (Write letters on small squares of paper or use Scrabble board game tiles.) Arrange the letters in a circle and place the glass in the center. Two people then sit with their fingers lightly touching the glass. Should the glass move, letters that it touches allegedly spell out messages. The use of a pendulum rather than a moving pointer enables a solitary person to consult a witch board without a partner.

CHAPTER 4

Arts and Crafts

If witches are "the ones who know," then exactly what is it that they know? What do witches *do* with this knowledge? What is this witchery all about? In order to fully understand the origins of witch lore, craft, and wisdom, we must envision an earlier era.

Imagine a primordial time. The earliest humans have migrated into new territories—the land is unfamiliar, resident plants and animals yet unknown. Imagine the critical questions: Does the land hold dangers? Is this a region prone to swamps? Earthquakes? Tornadoes? Do hidden sources of drinking water exist? What will we eat?

Crucially, people need to know which plants will heal which specific conditions as well as which plants will provide relief from pain or depression and which will provide a portal for ecstatic experiences. People need to know which plants will boost fertility when desired or suppress it in times of trouble. If you are inclined to acknowledge the existence of spirits, then you will appreciate that people need to identify local spirits and determine whether they are friendly or if not—then how they may be appeased.

Those who first coaxed secret information from Earth were the earliest witches. Witches developed deep, esoteric knowledge of plants, living creatures, and the spirit realms. They gazed up at stars and down at rocks, crawled into caves, and eventually, over millennia, developed occult arts and crafts. Witches evolved into healers, diviners, astrologers, ironworkers, ritualists, spell-casters, and more.

Thus, the witches' craft encompasses many forms of knowledge. The following are among the most famous, although other esoteric arts and crafts exist, too. Not every witch is familiar with every one of these topics, but each of these arts and crafts has traditionally been associated with witches.

Alchemy

Alchemy is the ancient art of transmutation. Does that sound dauntingly arcane? It is, and yet it isn't. If you have ever baked a cake from scratch, then you, too, have performed an alchemical feat of transmutation.

Synonyms for *transmute* include *transform* and *change*. To transmute is to take something and transform it into something completely different. The stereotypical alchemist, at least according to novels and movies, is a mad sorcerer hell-bent on transforming cheap, base metals into gold. But there is much more to alchemy than this.

Alchemy's roots are mysterious and primordial. Exactly how primordial? Some perceive that they lie in ancient metalworking traditions and that the very first metalworkers to develop alloys were the earliest alchemists. Alternatively, the first alchemists might be those revolutionary thinkers who first realized that grain could be transformed into beer and bread. That may sound arcane today, but imagine living during the pre-agricultural hunting-gathering era. What visionary looked at wheat or barley growing in the ground and realized the transmutations that were possible? Some scholars think that witchcraft's origins lie in what are described as "ancient grain cults."

Perhaps alchemy's roots may be traced even further back in time, to our primitive ancestors who first discovered the concept of "cooking," the transmutation of raw into cooked. The act of cooking is unique to humans; only people cook. Many anthropologists consider it the defining characteristic that distinguishes humans from all other animal species—yet another transmutation.

Transmutation and transformation may be metaphoric, too. Ignorance is transmuted into wisdom and enlightenment. A mere human may be transformed into a divine being. Those are the larger spiritual concerns that inspired classical alchemists.

The word *alchemy* is borrowed from an Arabic word meaning "the Egyptian science" or "the black art." Alchemy is the original "black art," but once upon a time that term did not hold the malevolent undertones it does today. The name *Egypt* is a Greek word. The name the ancient Egyptians actually called their own nation was *Kemet*, meaning "the black land," referring to Egypt's rich, black, alluvial soil. Black was considered the color of fertility, prosperity, abundance, health, safety, and regeneration.

Although many alchemists did strive to produce gold—it's what kings paid them to do—in general, the alchemist's true secret quest was for longevity or even immortality. Alchemists attempted to create the magical substance called the Philosopher's Stone, which, despite its name, is usually envisioned as a black powder or a wax or tincture. (The Chinese equivalent of the Philosopher's Stone is usually envisioned as a pill or elixir.) Other names for the Philosopher's

Stone include "Stone of the Sages" and "Powder of Projection." The first *Harry Potter* novel was published in the United Kingdom under the title *Harry Potter and the Philosopher's Stone*, but publishers, fearing that title was too erudite for American readers, renamed the US version *Harry Potter and the Sorcerer's Stone*.

The Philosopher's Stone can allegedly heal any illness, and promote longevity to the point of virtual immortality while simultaneously preserving or returning youth, health and vigor. In addition to these powers, the Philosopher's Stone can also reputedly transform cheap, base metals into gold, a crucial source of income for an immortal who will have to pay bills forever.

World-famous alchemists include Count Cagliostro, Dr. John Dee, and Nicholas Flamel, whose modern fame rests largely on his appearance in the *Harry Potter* novels but who reputedly really possessed the secret of the Philosopher's Stone.

Astrology

The most crucial astrological concept is expressed by the aphorism, *As above, so below.* This saying indicates that by studying, analyzing, and interpreting heavenly bodies like asteroids, planets, and stars, we are better able to understand and also accurately predict what will happen here on Earth. Astrology is the art of star-gazing, the science of the stars. Sybil Leek, astrologer, author, and witch, defined astrology as the influence of the planets on all living things. Many diverse schools of astrology exist. Classical Western astrology is based on ancient Babylonian and Greek traditions and incorporates twelve zodiac signs (Aries, Taurus, Gemini, Cancer, Leo, Virgo, Libra, Scorpio, Sagittarius, Capricorn, Aquarius, and Pisces). Other formal schools include Tibetan, Chinese, Mayan, Lakota, and Dogon astrology, as well as Vedic astrology from India.

Not every astrologer is a witch, and not every witch is an astrologer. However, even many witches who would not consider themselves formal astrologers still incorporate the basic tenets of astrological knowledge into their practice and daily lives, using astrology to help choose the most auspicious times to plan rituals, cast spells, and make important decisions. Simple, basic daily astrological information may be found in the annual publication *The Witches' Almanac*, as well as in other publications. Famed astrologer-witches include Dr. John Dee, Abei no Seimei, and Agrippa.

Botanical

Working with botanicals is the original, primordial, and preeminent witchly art. While many witches have no direct experience with astrology, divination, or alchemy, virtually *all* witches incorporate plants in some form into their craft.

Botanicals take many forms. The word *botanical* encompasses all kinds of plants: flowering plants, herbs, ferns, vines, trees, cacti—any sort of vegetation. Any part of a plant is considered a botanical, too: leaves, roots, stems, flowers, bulbs, or bark, for instance.

A botanical may be a living plant, but the word also encompasses dried and processed plants. Botanicals are transformed via different methods of processing into healing flower essences as well as fragrant essential oils, the integral components of aromatherapy. Botanicals are crafted into incense, smudge sticks, wreaths, and garlands, and are blended into perfume. Botanicals are added to candles, potions, enchanted baths, charm bags, and virtually every kind of magic spell. Botanicals are incorporated into sacred ritual.

Of course, one does not have to be a witch to have contact with botanicals. In fact, botanicals are so ever-present, they are difficult for anyone to avoid. If you begin your day with a cup of coffee, tea, orange juice, or cocoa, you begin your day with botanicals. If you eat salad or add pepper, ketchup, or hot sauce to your food, you are incorporating botanicals. Toast is but transformed grain. Unless you are a Breatharian or follow an exclusively carnivorous diet, you are a con-sumer of botanicals. When you walk on grass or accept a bouquet of flowers, you have contact with botanicals. Look in the closet: cotton t-shirts and linen pants are also botanical products, although they no longer look anything like plants.

For witches, however, botanicals possess far deeper significance. A basic magical tenet is that *all* plants possess some kind of power, whether to heal, harm, or both. Many possess profound magical attributes: using them in certain ways encourages romance or prosperity. Others are believed to provide spiritual protection, en-courage justice, or provide portals to Fairyland. For in-stance, allegedly the scent of cinnamon or frankincense consistently attracts powerful and benevolent spirits.

The earliest witches experimented. The process of spell-casting, then as now, involves a component of trial and error before one can determine what consistently works. According to the tenets of shamanism, the earliest magical practitioners learned how to communicate directly with plants and the spirits associated with plants, like devas. Through these communications, the complex power of each individual botanical was revealed, as well as what happens when you combine them.

These earliest witches shared and transmitted this knowledge to others, and it became the basis for herbal and magical traditions. Even now, modern Amazonian shamans describe similar experiences in which plants and plant spirits offer direct communication and instruction. Eventually, a huge trove of botanical knowledge was accumulated and passed down, sometimes in writing but most often orally. In the 21st century, much of this information is contained within books for all to learn. Among the witches famed for their knowledge of botanicals is Franz Bardon.

Divination

The art of seeing the future or the past in the present is known as divination. Through divination, one can better understand the past, foretell the future, and make better decisions right now. A diviner is someone who practices divination. Other names for this type of practitioner include seer or fortune-teller. Not all diviners consider themselves witches, but many witches practice divination.

Divination is not the same thing as being psychic, telepathic, or clairvoyant, although there are individuals who possess those talents and are also skilled diviners. A psychic *knows* things; a telepath can read minds (like the fictional characters Jean Grey of the X-Men or *True Blood*'s Sookie Stackhouse); a clairvoyant can "see" future events or current events happening in other places. Although some people work to acquire or refine these skills, others are just born with them. There may be no effort involved in being psychic. A vision is simply experienced. Many telepaths can't help themselves; they're not trying to read others' thoughts—it just happens.

Divination, on the other hand, is a learned skill that usually involves acquiring some sort of technique and learning to use some sort of tool, like runes or crystal balls. Other popular methods of divination include reading cards, tea leaves, and coffee grounds. Some people display a natural talent for divination and become accomplished very quickly; for others, it takes much work, time, and effort.

A skilled diviner can transform virtually *anything* into a divination tool. Kitchen witches may practice divination with everyday household objects. For instance, one method involves breaking a raw egg into a glass of water and then interpreting the patterns made by the floating egg. This technique may have been the magical act that triggered the 1692 Salem witch panic.

Famous witch-diviners include Dr. John, Sybil Leek and Eliphas Levi.

Dowsing

Dowsing is an ancient method of locating treasure hidden within the Earth. This treasure may take the form of sources of water, gemstones, metal, and mineral deposits. When the goal is finding water, dowsing is known as water witching. Dowsing may also be used to locate oil and missing bodies. This technique has been used to map archeological and underwater sites as well as to diagnose illness.

Some water witches are able to locate water using only their native psychic dowsing ability, but most incorporate a tool to help them dowse. The most common dowsing tool is a forked stick, known as a dowsing rod, wizard rod, or Y-rod (because its shape resembles a letter Y). Other dowsing tools include bent wire, pendulums, and wooden rods of other shapes.

Dowsers may incorporate secret, ritual knowledge when handcrafting tools to increase their power and efficacy. Individual dowsers may favor specific types of wood: hazel, rowan, or willows are favorites, for instance—all trees historically associated with witches and fairies.

Wood for dowsing tools may be obtained via magical rituals. The tree may be asked for permission before a branch is cut, and gifts may be offered to the tree in reciprocation. Alternatively, the branch must be taken only from a certain direction on the tree, or must be found already fallen on the ground in a specific location. Rituals may be incorporated into preparing the tool, too.

The earliest documentation of what appears to be dowsing dates back to the Cro-Magnon era and appears in cave paintings in what is now modern Spain. Dowsing tools were also found in the tomb of Pharaoh Tutankhamun in Egypt. Although once considered a simple, practical function, by the 15th century, dowsing had become associated with witches in Europe. Protestant reformer Martin Luther called dowsing the work of the devil.

Dowsing is used to locate the metaphysical as well as the tangible: telluric currents and ley lines, but also land mines and subterranean tunnels. World famous dowsers include Leonardo da Vinci and Albert Einstein.

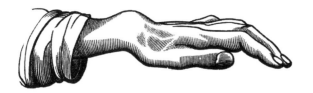

Healing

Among the original, primordial magical crafts, healing remains an important magical art. Then as now, healers prescribed botanical cures, diagnosed illness via divination and shamanic journey, and used magical techniques to safeguard the health of individuals and communities. The ability to heal is often considered proof that someone possesses magical power. Many consider faith-healing to be but one step from witchcraft.

During the witch hunt era, healers were especially targeted as witches. People who were believed to cause illness were prosecuted as witches, but so were those who healed and produced cures. Traditional healers were accused of causing illness so that they would then be hired to heal it, for the purpose of financial gain.

In Europe as elsewhere, a high percentage of traditional healers have historically been female. Close associations between women, witches, and healers may have been among the sparks of Europe's centuries-long witch panic. The ability to heal an ailment, especially when it had stymied a licensed male physician, was considered evidence of witchcraft. (Only men could then be licensed as physicians.) Many healers were swept up in the witchcraze, whether or not they genuinely were witches.

Modern witches remain involved with healing of body, mind, and soul. Many witches are accomplished herbalists, aromatherapists, flower essence practitioners, massage therapists, and reiki masters. Among the witches and occultists renowned as healers are Agrippa, Franz Bardon, and Marie Laveau.

Metalworking

The profession most profoundly associated with the magical arts is metalworking, especially ironworking. The history of witches is intertwined with the history of smithcraft. Smiths—ancient alchemists—evolved the art of transmutation, transforming one substance into another (iron into steel, for instance). Details of smithcraft were kept secret for centuries. Those who knew these secrets were able to craft weapons and tools that could be used to successfully dominate others, militarily or magically.

Metal is dug from deep within Earth, and magic spells and rituals, closely held family secrets, were performed to appease fierce guardian spirits. Metalworkers evolved into the original master magicians, priestesses, and priests of Earth's mysteries. Iron, almost universally considered the most magically potent metal, comes from an additional and unique source: meteorites that fall from the sky. Metalworkers, thus, were considered privy to the secrets of Heaven and Earth.

Magical smith clans evolved, simultaneously respected and feared by their neighbors. Because their magic tricks were kept secret, smiths became the first professional magicians, requested and paid to perform rituals and cast spells for the benefit of others. Historically ironworkers do more than forge steel: they also serve their communities as healers, tattoo artists, and herbal practitioners. Smiths carve amulets and craft magical as well as agricultural or military tools. Witchcraft tools are not only forged, but also ritually prepared and blessed, another service provided by the ironworker.

This tradition of the magical ironworker took place wherever iron was present, and it continues today. Among the modern witches associated with metalworking is Robert Cochrane, founder of the Clan of Tubal Cain. Deities associated with both witchcraft and ironcraft include Africa's Ogun.

Necromancy

Any word ending with the suffix *-mancy* refers to some kind of divination. Thus, *cartomancy* is another word for card reading, *chiromancy* for palm reading, and *tasseomancy* for tea leaf reading. Necromancy is divination via the dead.

No need to grab a shovel. Necromancy is not a synonym for grave desecration. Most methods of necromancy do not involve any contact with dead bodies. Most necromancy is accomplished via divination techniques. If you have ever consciously tried to contact a dead loved one in dreams or via a séance or Ouija board, then you too have engaged in necromancy. You, too, are a necromancer.

Historically, the word *necromancer* has been used as a synonym for *sorcerer*, regardless of whether any actual necromancy is involved. The most famous true necromancers are Greek goddess Circe and the Bible's Woman of Endor. Witch goddesses Freya and Oya preside over necromantic rituals. Magicians Agrippa and Dr. John Dee are often described as necromancers. Dr. Orpheus, a character from the popular animated television series, *The Venture Brothers*, identifies himself as a necromancer.

# Scrying

The meanings of cards and runes may be memorized, but scrying is a totally intuitive art. Scrying is a form of divination that involves the art of gazing. One gazes into a smooth surface until visions begin to appear, either on the surface itself or in the mind's eye.

Crystal ball gazing is the most famous form of scrying, but mirrors and other items are also used. An ancient scrying technique includes gazing into a highly polished thumb nail. Any clear surface potentially serves as a scrying tool: polished metal, for instance, or even a pan of water. The precious cup that the biblical Joseph accused his brothers of stealing was his special divining chalice.

Eurasian witch goddess Kybele is frequently depicted gazing into a pan of water, indicating her oracular skill. The Aztec obsidian mirror used by Dr. John Dee to scry and communicate with angels is now housed in the British Museum.

Sigils

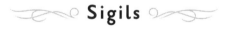

Also known as seals, sigils are geometric or visual designs typically enclosed in a circle and created for spiritual and magical purposes. Sigils are incorporated into spell-casting, spirit communication, and are used to make protective talismans. If you have ever seen a television character—for example, one of the Winchester brothers of the CW series *Supernatural*—draw elaborate, highly detailed designs within circles with the intent of trapping, banishing, or luring a demon, then you have seen something akin to a sigil.

Many of the sigils incorporated into classical Western Ceremonial Magic date back to at least the time of King Solomon, ancient Israel's wizard king. Traditions similar to these sigils exist worldwide. Examples include Vodou vèvès and Pennsylvania Dutch hex signs. (*Hex* means "witch" in German; a hex sign is literally a *witch sign*.) The magic of author and artist Austin Osman Spare incorporates sigils.

Spell-Casting

The *craft* referred to in witch*craft* is usually considered to be spell-casting or spellcraft. Many people would define "witch" as a synonym for spell-caster. Although rarely accompanied by the special effects that signal successful spell-craft in television and movies (Lights! Smoke! Noise!), real spell-casting is an art, not make believe.

The art of spell-casting posits that everything that exists radiates some sort of magical energy. Iron, silver, frankincense, and myrrh radiate protection. Roses offer healing powers and beckon love, while green, leafy plants are used to increase prosperity. Every material, fragrance, color—virtually anything you can think of—possesses some sort of power. Different times of the year are conducive to different kinds of spells: the autumn and winter seasons, for instance, are considered ideal for communicating with the dearly departed, while Midsummer's Eve is ideal for love magic.

Witches are the ones who know the information crucial for successful spell-casting—or, at the very least, they know where to find it. A magic spell may be defined as a formalized conscious attempt to harness and manipulate these magical energies in order to achieve a spell-caster's goal. Spells may be cast for any goal. If you can conceive of it, a spell exists to attain it. Spells take many forms and styles, from the incredibly elaborate and highly ritualized to the simplest little word charm. The tradition of making a wish and blowing out birthday candles derives from an old spell, as does the custom of wishing on a star or full moon.

⚬ Spirit Working ⚬

A vast variety of spirits will communicate and work with people, including angels, fairies, saints, deities of all types, ghosts, and ancestors. Spirit working is the magical art of communicating with them. By communicating with spirits, one can form partnerships and alliances, request favors, and express gratitude, love, and veneration for them. Beneficial spirits can be welcomed, while scary spirits like nasty ghosts can be asked to leave. If unpleasant spirits are uncooperative, then more powerful spirits may be requested to forcibly evict them. Spirits like Hekate and Oya, for instance, will reputedly remove harmful or annoying ghosts.

Spirit working derives from shamanism. A spirit worker is an independent practitioner who is in direct personal communication with spirits. This may be accomplished via different methods, including divination. Spirit working does not involve ritual possession. The spirit worker is completely conscious, although communication may also be accomplished in dreams and guided visualization. Among the many famous spirit workers are Dr. John Dee and Marie Laveau.

CHAPTER 5

Divine Witches

Yes, witches have been feared and persecuted, but they
have also been worshipped. Deities that fit the definition of witches are venerated around the world and
by many different spiritual traditions. Many are explicitly identified as witches in their sacred mythology.
Although any spirit may possess supernatural powers,
divine witches cast spells and otherwise behave like human witches. Many also serve as sponsors or guardians
for human witches, offering magical instruction and
sometimes bestowing added magic power.

    Christianity demonized all Pagan spirits, regardless
of whether they were originally perceived as benevolent
or dangerous. All Pagan spirits were considered subversive, but the ones considered most diabolical were

those associated with witches and magical practice. Some considered the Norse deity Odin to be the devil, for instance, while spirits like Freya or Hekate served as prototypes for stereotypes of human witches: Freya as the alluring, seductive femme fatale and Hekate as a decrepit old hag.

The list and description of spirits that follows is but a sampling of some of the most famous and influential divine witches. Many remain actively venerated or survive in fairy tales and folktales. They derive from different pantheons and several continents. Although all are associated with witches, they are not all the same type of spirit. Genres of spirits represented here include fairies, mermaids, and orishas.

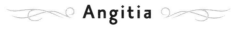

Angitia

Angitia, Circe's granddaughter, is a snake-charming sorceress goddess originally venerated by the Marsi, a tribe that inhabited central Italy before they were conquered and absorbed by the Romans. The Marsi traced their lineage from a son of Circe. Angitia, their primary deity, was his daughter and thus also an ancestral goddess.

Angitia had a temple and a sacred grove on the shores of Lake Fucino. Archaeological excavations have revealed artifacts that were dedicated to her before being tossed in the lake. Another version of her myth suggests that after Medea was forced to flee from

Greece, she traveled to Italy, where she assumed the identity of the snake-handling goddess of healing and magic, Angitia.

Worship of Angitia was suppressed, initially by the Romans after their victory over the Marsi, and then by Christian authorities who banished all Pagan religions. However, some of her rituals survive. They are now dedicated to San Domenico, a saint venerated in territories once associated with the Marsi and who is believed to demonstrate miraculous healing powers, especially over snakebites. His feast, which features snake-handling, is celebrated in the Italian village of Cocullo on the first Thursday in May.

 **Aradia**

The star of the mysterious book *Aradia or The Gospel of the Witches*, is Aradia, the Messiah of the Witches. Author and folklorist Charles Godfrey Leland (1824–1903) was in Italy researching traditional witchcraft practices when on New Year's Day, 1897, one of his paid sources, a fortune-teller named Maddelena, brought him a handwritten copy she had made of what she said was an older manuscript.

This manuscript, which became Leland's famous *Aradia or The Gospel of the Witches*, retells the history of the world.

According to *Aradia*, in the beginning there was Diana, the primordial Spirit of Darkness. Diana

  The Weiser Field Guide to Witches

divided the world into complementary opposites: light and dark, male and female. The light half evolved into her brother Lucifer (whose name literally means "light bringer"). Diana took the form of a black cat and seduced him, and from this union Aradia, the first witch, was conceived. Diana sent her daughter to Earth with the express command to teach people the sacred arts of witchcraft.

That's the first incarnation of Aradia. She had a second coming, too. This second Aradia was born on August 13, 1313 in Volterra, Italy. (August 13 is the date of Diana's ancient Roman festival.) She learned the Old Ways from her family, then proceeded to evangelize, teaching them to others, and in the process sparking a revival of Italian witchcraft and pre-Christian Italian spirituality. Captured by the Inquisition, she was burned as a witch—but not before leaving a written testament, which was secretly handed down for generations before arriving in Leland's hands.

Both the legend of Aradia and the publication of the book remain extremely controversial. Leland himself wasn't sure how much of the manuscript he received was copied from another and how much was based on oral traditions. He translated the Italian into English, added commentary, and published the book in London in 1899.

No other copies of a manuscript resembling *Aradia* have ever been found. The story of Diana as world creatrix and mother of the first witch appears nowhere else. However, many myths are derived from one version of a text: lack of corroborating evidence does not in itself prove that Leland's manuscript is fraudulent. While scholars argue about the myth's legitimacy, the goddess Aradia has been embraced by many Wiccans, witches, and goddess devotees. She now ranks among the most popular modern goddesses, and many devotees have testified to having personally experienced her blessings and presence.

Baba Yaga

Deep within a primordial Russian birch forest is a little hut containing a huge stove. This house stands on giant chicken legs. It's a mobile home—approach, and it might scurry away. If you want admittance, however, just chant the not-so-secret formula: *Izbushka, Izbushka, turn around and let me in. Izbushka* literally means "little hut," and if you say the chant, the house will do as you ask. This house belongs to Baba Yaga, a fierce cannibal witch and the star of Russian fairy-tales.

For years, Russian children have been warned to stay out of the woods, lest Baba Yaga eat them. Baba Yaga has iron teeth and boar tusks. Although she has a broom, she doesn't ride it. Instead Baba Yaga rides within a mortar, steers with the pestle, and uses the broom to sweep her traces away so that no one can tell where she's been.

Baba Yaga is the protective guardian of all forest creatures. Harm them and fear her wrath. She is the genius of the forest who knows the magical and medicinal uses of every plant on Earth—and then some! Allegedly, there is no illness she cannot cure—*if* she so chooses.

Scholars suggest that legends of Baba Yaga are vestigial memories of an ancient great goddess, perhaps Russian, perhaps Scythian. Her myths have devolved into fairy tales, and her stove may be understood as the cauldron of regeneration associated with other ancient shamanic goddesses such as Cerridwen or Medea.

 ## Cerridwen

This great sorceress is a Celtic lunar goddess and keeper of the Cauldron of Wisdom, Information, and Transformation. Cerridwen is a brilliant shapeshifter who can take any form, although her favorites are allegedly those of a woman or a great white sow.

Cerridwen's primary surviving myth appears in the *Book of Taliesin*, a 13th-century manuscript named for the 6th-century Welsh poet, prophet, and bard. In this myth, Cerridwen fears that her beloved son lacks the innate gifts to be successful, and so she determines to brew a special potion just for him. Once tasted, this potion bestows all wisdom, knowledge, magical power, and oracular and shamanic skill. Cerridwen alone knows the formula.

Concocting it is no easy feat. A tremendous quantity of botanicals must be gathered, each at just the right moment, in the right quantity and with the correct ritual. Each ingredient must be added to the cauldron at exactly the right moment and in the right order. Furthermore, the potion must be stirred continuously for a year and a day before it is ready.

Cerridwen captures Gwion, a young orphan, and forces him to serve as her potion stirrer. Cerridwen, who adores her own children, shows no mercy for the orphan, treating him abusively, feeding him as little as possible, and forcing as much labor out of him as she can.

As the year and a day draw to a close, the liquid in the bubbling cauldron splatters, scalding Gwion's hand. Perhaps the starved orphan finally got careless; perhaps he was blessed by constant proximity to Cerridwen's magical cauldron. Sticking his finger in his mouth to ease the pain, Gwion becomes the recipient of the cauldron's gifts. Suddenly, with that brief taste of the potion, he literally knows all! Instantly transforming into a master magician, he realizes that Cerridwen intends to kill him. (The potion is a single serving. It can only benefit one. Having received its gifts, Gwion—the future Taliesin—has supplanted Cerridwen's son, the intended recipient.)

Gwion flees, transforming into forms he hopes will disguise him. Cerridwen pursues, transforming in turn. If he becomes a fish, she becomes a bigger one. If he transforms into a bird, she becomes a raptor, chasing him through the air. Finally, he transforms into a grain of wheat. Cerridwen, in the guise of a hen, gobbles him up.

But Gwion does not disappear. Instead, he gestates in her womb so that Cerridwen herself becomes a magical cauldron of regeneration. Although initially determined to destroy him as soon as he is born, the baby she births is so radiantly beautiful that she cannot kill him. This re-born soul, still in possession of all magical knowledge, will become the prophet Taliesin, whose name means "shining brow" in Middle Welsh.

Circe

The sorceress goddess Circe lives in a luxurious marble palazzo on a mysterious Mediterranean island named Aiaia. (It's also spelled Aeaea; ancient Greek magical theory suggests that vowels have tremendous magic power.) She most famously appears in Homer's *Odyssey*; Homer refers to her in language that clearly identifies her as among the great goddesses, not merely a mortal sorceress or even a demi-goddess. Her feats are magical: Circe transforms men into animals—usually pigs, but, depending on the nature of the man, sometimes lions or baboons, too.

In the *Odyssey*, the Greek hero Odysseus and his crew run into adventure after adventure in their attempt to return home following the end of the Trojan War. When their ship lands on Aiaia, an island previously unknown to them, the crew—minus Odysseus—goes exploring. An encounter with Circe results in their transformation into swine.

With a little magical assistance from the Greek god Hermes, Odysseus is able to forge an alliance with Circe and rescue his transformed men. Odysseus lives with Circe for ten years, engaged in a passionate love affair, but also learning her magical skills. When he finally leaves, she gives him explicit, detailed instructions for safely navigating the rest of his journey, including a pit stop in Hades. Suffice it to say, without Circe, Odysseus would never have reached home.

Circe appears in other Greek myths, too. She poisons the water in which a perceived romantic rival swims, magically transforming the beautiful sea goddess Scylla into the sea monster that will later terrorize Odysseus' ship. Circe also performs the purification rituals that spiritually cleanse Medea and Jason after their murder of Medea's brother in the epic of The Golden Fleece.

For centuries, Circe, the beautiful, dangerous, magical femme fatale, has been a crowd pleaser and the inspiration for much popular entertainment. She was the subject of the very first ballet, staged in 1581 in Paris, possibly as a tribute to French Queen Catherine de Medici, long rumored to be a sorceress. Circe was a great favorite of Renaissance and Victorian artists alike. John William Waterhouse created several famous portraits of her, including *Circe Invidiosa* and *Circe Offering the Cup to Ulysses*. Other artists inspired by Circe include Edward Burne-Jones, John Collier, and Franz von Stuck.

Circe also makes frequent appearances in modern comics, notably as Wonder Woman's nemesis. As Sersi, a member of the celestial super-race, the Eternals, she was briefly a member of Captain America's Avengers and, ever the charmer, romantically involved with Captain America himself.

Diana

Few spirits are more closely associated with witches than the goddess Diana. A spirit of the forest, wild nature, women, magic, and the moon, Diana is a particularly ancient, indigenous Italian goddess whose roots in Italy are far older than those of the Romans. In other words, when the Romans arrived in Italy, they found Diana already there. Scholars suspect that she was once the preeminent Italian female deity but that the Romans, who possessed an intensely patriarchal culture, were uncomfortable with autonomous women and unrestricted practice of the magical arts, both associated with Diana. Her place in the Roman pantheon would eventually be assumed by Juno.

Worship of Diana continued, however. She presided over a temple shrine on the shores of Lake Nemi, and had a temple on Rome's Aventine Hill. Women, slaves, and immigrants constituted a large percentage of her devotees; thus, from the perspective of an authoritarian state, she was perceived as a subversive goddess long before the emergence of Christianity. Roman soldiers carried veneration of Diana throughout Europe, once a densely forested continent. Diana worship spread throughout Celtic regions as well as central and eastern Europe, especially in what are now Poland, Serbia, and Transylvania.

Over the centuries, Diana has become intensely associated with the Greek goddess Artemis; their names are frequently used interchangeably even though his-

torically they are distinct goddesses. Both are moon goddesses associated with wild nature, women, and the magical arts. Diana's associations with witchcraft are stronger than those of Artemis, and there is less focus on chastity in Diana's mythos.

Worship of Diana was banned following Rome's official conversion to Christianity, but it never vanished. She continued to be venerated in secret nocturnal rites. The Inquisition considered Diana among the spirits most closely associated with witches, who were accused of belonging to the "Society of Diana."

Diana continues to reign as Queen of the Night and is beloved by both modern goddess devotees and practitioners of the Italian witchcraft tradition, Stregheria.

Freya

The most beautiful spirit of the entire Nordic pantheon, Freya has dominion over love, sex, magic, divination, fertility, war, happiness, and witches, too. Once venerated over a huge swathe of northern Europe, golden Freya most typically manifests as a gorgeous woman, but she owns a falcon feather cloak that enables her to fly like a falcon and shape-shift into any form she desires.

Freya rides a boar into battle. On non-military occasions, she drives a chariot drawn by two huge grey cats, her sacred creatures. (They may be big Norwegian forest cats or lynxes.) The day Friday is named in her honor: it is her sacred day. Freya's sacred number is thirteen, the number of months in a lunar year. One theory regarding why Friday the 13th is perceived as unlucky is that, for centuries, Church propaganda discouraged affection for that day as it indicated affection for Freya.

Freya presides over life and death. Surviving myths indicate that people prayed to her for children and enhanced fertility. As leader of the Valkyries, Freya presides over battlefields, choosing half the dead to come live with her forever in her luxurious hall. (The other half spend the afterlife with Odin.) Freya also presides over the shamanic arts, especially *seior*, the women's art of foretelling the future and communicating with souls in the afterlife. Whether because of her powerful associations with witchcraft, because she was so seductive, or just because people loved her so much, no Nordic spirit was so despised by the Church as Freya. Ironically, much historic information regarding Freya survives, precisely because the Church hated her so much and recorded their opposition in detail. Freya's last surviving temple in what is now Magdeburg, Germany was closed by an edict of Charlemagne, but active veneration of Freya survived, allegedly into the 17th century. She is currently among the most beloved Neo-Pagan goddesses.

Gran Ibo

A goddess in the guise of an old swamp witch, Gran Ibo knows all the secrets of the swamp. Gran Ibo is a master herbalist and magical practitioner. She commands alligators and snakes. She knows the mysteries of all plants and can teach them to you.

An ancient African spirit, possibly Congolese, Gran Ibo traveled to the Western Hemisphere with the slave trade. A solitary spirit, she made herself at home in the swamps of the Caribbean and Louisiana. She is the matron and prototype of swamp witches, a repository of boundless mysteries and information.

Gran Ibo has been described as a goddess of patience and wisdom; she is a watchful spirit who observes and analyzes all. Whatever information she cannot find by herself is brought to her by messenger birds. Her special familiar is a canary who whispers secrets in her ear, alerting her of any approaching danger.

Gran Ibo is venerated in the Vodou traditions of Haiti and New Orleans. Her image appears on one of the divinatory cards in *The New Orleans Voodoo Tarot* by Louis Martinié and Sallie Ann Glassman.

Hekate

Queen of the Crossroads and Goddess of Night, Hekate, also spelled Hecate, is now most closely associated with Greek mythology. But her name, meaning "Influence from Afar," acknowledges her foreign origins. An ancient, primordial spirit, she may originally have come from what is now modern Turkey or Georgia, on the Black Sea. Once upon a time, as recorded in the Greek myth of Jason and the Golden Fleece, Hekate was worshipped in a great temple surrounded by lavish botanical gardens in Colchis, in what is now modern Georgia.

Hekate is a goddess of life *and* death, fertility, wisdom, choices, magic, victory, vengeance, justice, and travel. She is at home in the realms of life and death. This dark moon goddess patrols the frontier between those realms, providing access to those shamans who seek to travel between, or placing obstacles in their path. Hekate can provide safe travel to any realm and on any road, in any dimension. She serves as a psychopomp, providing escort service so that dead souls arrive safely in the appropriate afterlife realm.

Hekate's most famous appearance in Greek myth is in the epic saga of Persephone's abduction. When Persephone's mother Demeter, seeks assistance in finding her stolen daughter, only Hekate volunteers her help. (Hekate is allegedly the witness to every crime. She may be invoked for justice and assistance.)

Hekate is a shape-shifter with the power to take any form. Although often depicted as an old crone or hag, she is just as likely to assume the guise of a beautiful, sensuous woman. Her love affairs, as recorded in mythology, are legion. Hekate frequently manifests as a black dog, but she can also assume the form of a black cat, a black sow, or a dragon.

Hekate's sacred number is three. Her color is black. Brooms, keys, cauldrons, and torches are among her

The Weiser Field Guide to Witches

emblems. Dragons pull her chariot. Her sacred creatures include dragons, toads, snakes, bats, and cats, but especially dogs. Dogs serve as her messengers. Hekate is the guardian of all dogs, not only black dogs. She may be invoked for protection *for* dogs and also *from* dogs.

Hekate's most famous theatrical appearance is in Shakespeare's *Macbeth*. Rather than fading into obscurity, Hekate is the object of ever-increasing veneration from goddess devotees and Neo-Pagans. There are several Facebook groups dedicated to her.

Hsi Wang Mu

Known as The Queen Mother of the West or as the Western Mother, Hsi Wang Mu is China's goddess of shamanism, sorcery, magic, alchemy, birth, death, and esoteric wisdom. She is the Queen of the Western Paradise, a Chinese afterlife realm populated by fairies and other spirits, where she serves as the keeper and guardian of the Peaches of Immortality. Eat them and live forever. Hsi Wang Mu decides who gets to eat those peaches. She has the power to bestow immortality and maintains a registry of all alchemists who have attained eternal life.

Hsi Wang Mu is a mediator between people, spirits, and ghosts. She is the presiding goddess of shamans and alchemists of all genders, but also specifically of women who lead unconventional lives, including witches, priestesses, fortune-tellers, and mystical adepts. She presides over sacred arts including meditation, visualization, Tantra, alchemy, and magical and healing potions and elixirs.

Scholars consider Hsi Wang Mu to be the oldest surviving Chinese goddess. She may originally have been a deified tribal ancestor and shamanic leader of a northwestern tribal people. Eventually, after evolving into a powerful goddess and extending her terrain, Hsi Wang Mu was adopted into the early Taoist pantheon.

The various creatures with which she is most closely associated (tigers, magpies, crows, foxes) all have profound associations with witches, magic, and sorcery. Hsi Wang Mu often appears accompanied by packs of tigers and leopards. She may ride a white tiger or appear in the guise of one. The rabbit in the moon is her servant. Hsi Wang Mu also has powerful associations with the legendary nine-tailed fox.

Hulda

When Hulda shakes her featherbed, snow falls on Earth. Rain is her laundry rinse water. Fog hovering over a mountain may be smoke from her hearth fires. Snow Queen and weather goddess Hulda, also known as Frau Holle or Mother Holle, is an ancient Teutonic deity of birth and death. She presides over a crossroads realm that straddles the boundaries of life and death and which essentially serves as a transit station for human souls. Hulda receives the souls of the newly dead into her realm and releases souls to be newly born again. She is a goddess of death, fertility, and witchcraft. She leads a band of forest fairies. Depending on the version of her myth, Hulda may be the Elf Queen.

Mountain caves and elder trees serve as portals to her realm. (That's elder tree as in the Latin classification *Sambucus nigra*, source of elderberries and commonly called the "witch tree"—not just any well-aged tree.) Her realm may also be accessed via wells, as occurs in *Mother Holle*, the Brothers Grimm fairy tale in which she stars. She guards and nurtures all the growing things of the forest.

Hulda was once a preeminent northern European goddess. Holland is her namesake. Banished following the advent of Christianity, veneration of Hulda was forbidden on pain of death. (Those who disobeyed were branded witches.) Hulda was re-classified as a demon witch-goddess who attacked and harmed children. Children were cautioned that if they weren't obedient, Hulda would "get" them. Parents were warned that if unbaptized babies died, they would end up in Hulda's realm, not Christian Heaven.

A defiant spirit, Hulda did not disappear quietly, but instead emerged as a prominent witch goddess, riding out on stormy winter nights with the Wild Hunt, that dangerous and dreaded parade of spirits, often in the company of her good friend and sometimes paramour, Odin. Witches were rumored to dance and ride with Hulda and her fairies. She retained her storm-raising powers and was blamed for bad weather.

Depending on her mood, Hulda manifests as a fierce old crone with big teeth or as a radiantly beautiful blonde. She may also appear as a woman when seen from the front but a tree from behind. Hulda often appears walking alongside rivers or dancing down mountain paths, either alone or with an entourage of elves, fairies, and capering rabbits.

Isis

Titles that the Egyptians bestowed upon this beloved goddess include She Who is Rich in Spells, Great of Sorcery, Speaker of Spells, and the Great Witch. Isis,

the Mistress of Magic, possesses all magical secrets. She even knows the ultra-secret Ineffable Name of the Creator of the Universe, which serves as the key to the most powerful magic of all. With the command of this name, there is nothing Isis cannot accomplish, no miracle she cannot perform or gift she cannot bestow.

Although Isis is most closely associated with

Egypt, she was an international goddess who was worshipped from deep in east Africa through western Asia and into Europe as far as London's Thames River. The city of Paris was once dedicated to her. Some scholars think that the name Paris derives from the name Isis. (*Isis* is the Greek variant of her name. Her original Egyptian name is *Au Set*.)

Isis and her twin brother, Osiris, fell in love in the womb. Their saga is among the most popular romantic tragedies of all time. While Osiris invents the arts of civilization (agriculture, viniculture, ethics, and the building of cities) and travels the globe teaching these arts, Isis remains home mastering every occult art until she is the most powerful witch in existence.

In her myths, Isis is shown casting spells, uttering incantations, shape-shifting, re-membering dismembered bodies, magically healing venomous scorpion stings, and raising the dead, at least temporarily. Crocodiles, snakes, and scorpions do her bidding. Isis provides fertility, cures the sick, and protects travelers at sea. She can appear in any guise that she chooses.

Kapo

This goddess of witchery, occult power, and prophesy was venerated throughout the Hawaiian Islands but especially on the Isle of Molokai, once renowned for its community of powerful sorcerers. Kapo is simultaneously adored, respected, and feared. She is a powerful and unpredictable spirit who rules fertility, childbirth, miscarriage, abortion, and death. She has the power to break or reverse any hex or curse.

Kapo is among the preeminent spirits of hula dancing, whose roots lie in sacred ritual. Some legends credit her as hula's inventor. Like other Hawaiian deities, Kapo is a shape-shifter who can manifest in any form that she chooses: animal, botanical, mineral, or human. She can be terrifying or beautiful or both. Among Kapo's arsenal of magic tricks is a detachable flying vagina that she flings and retrieves at will. The imprint of her flying vagina may be seen on the eastern side of the hill Kohelepelepe (literally *detached vagina*) at Koko Head, Oahu.

Kapo's sacred creature is the eel. Her cousin, friend, and sometime traveling partner is Pelé, the famous volcano goddess who is also a formidable witch.

Kybele

A clay statue excavated at Catal Hayuk, located in what is now modern Turkey and dated from between six to eight thousand years old, depicts a woman flanked by leopards. Although it was discovered without name plate or inscription, it is recognizably an image of the goddess Kybele. In one form or another, the veneration of Kybele, also spelled Cybele, may have endured longer than that of any other divinity.

Before she was a goddess, Kybele was a forest witch. According to her myth, Kybele was an unwanted child, possibly a princess, left exposed in the wilderness. Instead of consuming her, leopards and lions raised and nurtured her; a leopard served as her wet-nurse. Living alone with the animals, Kybele became a witch so powerful that she evolved into an immortal goddess.

Kybele rules healing, witchcraft, fertility, women, and children. Her rituals, held in caves and forests, included ecstatic dancing, intoxication, music, and sacred sex. Her worship eventually emerged from forest caves and spread. Kybele was venerated in Rome and throughout Europe. The city of Lyons, France was dedicated to her. In urban areas, her cult had a high percentage of elite intellectuals, but she also remained very popular among the poorer classes.

The early Christian Church perceived Kybele's religion as strong competition and brutally suppressed it. Among other reasons, the Church despised Kybele for the prominence of women, homosexuals, lesbians, and the transgendered among her clergy. Although her veneration was widespread, none of her temples remain. Some ruins in Turkey may be visited. Saint Peter's Basilica in the Vatican was built directly over Kybele's Roman temple, and allegedly remnants may survive under the foundation. Veneration of Kybele was never totally suppressed, and she remains a favorite of independent practitioners and goddess devotees.

Lilith

The very name of this ancient spirit has become synonymous with "witch," although she is often also depicted as a vampire, demon, or succubus. (Traditional Jewish angelology classifies Lilith as an Angel of Prostitution.) Lilith appears in Sumerian, Babylonian, Assyrian, Canaanite, Hebrew, Mandaean, Persian, Sabaean, and Arabic myth and folklore. She may linger in Christianity under the guise of some Black Madonnas. She is omnipresent in Jewish myth, fairy tales, and folklore. A Yiddish term for "witches" is "Daughters of Lilith."

Jewish tradition suggests that Lilith is Adam's first wife, the true first woman, created not from Adam's rib but from Earth simultaneously with him. Poet and painter Dante Gabriel Rossetti described Lilith as "The witch he loved before the gift of Eve."

Adam and Lilith's relationship quickly became contentious. She refused to be subservient to him, specifically refusing to always lie beneath him during sex. Lilith demanded to be treated as an equal rather than a subordinate, basing her claim on their common origin. When Adam attempted to use force, Lilith uttered the secret Ineffable Name of the Creator and flew away from the Garden of Eden, initiating the first divorce. She hid in caves by the Red Sea. Powerful angels were sent to strong-arm her, forcing her to return to Eden, but her magic was too powerful. The angels returned empty-handed, and God, acceding to Lilith's desire not to return, created Eve so that Adam wouldn't be lonely.

Lilith is a shape-shifter who can take many forms, appearing as an old crone, a sexy woman, a black cat, a black dog, a bat, or an owl, her sacred bird and messenger. Christian legend suggests that Lilith was the snake in paradise who tempted Eve with the apple, although whether this was because of hostility toward her successor or because she genuinely wished to help Eve by feeding her knowledge remains a subject for debate.

A spirit of the night, Lilith has dominion over sexual desire, erotic dreams, and sacred sex magic. Although she has historically been blamed for miscarriage, stillbirth, crib death (SIDS), and infertility, legends suggest that Lilith the baby killer can bestow fertility when and if she chooses. Some legends depict her as a powerful guardian spirit.

No spirit exerts more fascination over media and popular culture than Lilith. Her appearances are genuinely too numerous to count. Lilith herself, or characters named in her honor or inspired by her, appear on stage, screen, and television as well as in books. She plays a prominent role in Goethe's *Faust*. A demon named Lilith threatens the world in the CW television series *Supernatural*. The subject of many paintings, Lilith was a great favorite of Pre-Raphaelite artists like John Collier and Dante Gabriel Rossetti.

Medea

Greek mythology presents Medea as an enchantress, witch, high priestess, and shaman. She is a spell-caster, a potions master, an herbalist, and a snake charmer. Medea comes from a prominent family. She served as high priestess in the temple of her aunt, Hekate. Another aunt is super sorceress Circe. Hekate and Circe are clearly divine, but Medea's own status is unclear. She may be a mortal or an eventually deified mortal, but some suggest that she was always a deity, just not one from the Olympian pantheon. The murders with which she is associated may be vestigial memories of human sacrifices.

Medea's chief claim to fame derives from her leading role in the Greek myth of Jason and the Golden Fleece.

She is the one who actually accomplishes Jason's various tasks and enables him to steal the Golden Fleece. Her alleged actions at the end of that Greek myth—she is accused of killing her sons, possibly to protect them but also possibly to spite their father who had betrayed her by marrying a Greek princess—are what has led to her near universal notoriety as a famous villain.

Of course, although the myth is Greek, Medea is not. She was a Georgian princess from Colchis, a place the Greeks then associated with the very ends of the world. The Greeks did not perceive her associations with witchcraft as glamorous, but rather as threatening, frightening, and foreign.

Although Medea may be a villain elsewhere, she is a goddess in Georgia, whose people scoff at the notion that Medea would kill her children. A Georgian legend suggests that the boys escaped with Medea. Another says that although her sons did die, Medea wasn't the killer. Instead they were killed by Corinthians, who perceived Medea's sons as rivals for Jason's future Greek children.

There are many versions of Medea's fate. In one version she commits suicide, but usually Medea does not die. Instead she escapes in a chariot pulled by dragons. One myth claims that Medea escaped to Italy, where she assumed the identity of snake charmer goddess Angitia. Another claims that Medea now rules an afterlife realm together with Greek hero Achilles, her new husband.

Medea has long been a popular culture favorite. She starred in at least ten Greek and Latin plays, although only two survive in more than fragmentary form. Medea's myth is preserved in Euripides' play *Medea*, first produced in 431 BC. In addition to many other films, books, and plays, Medea appears as a maligned heroine in German author Christa Wolf's 1998 novel, *Medea*.

Morgan Le Fey

Now most famous for her role as King Arthur's rival, half-sister, and sometimes lover, Morgan Le Fey, sometimes called Morgana Le Fey, is, in fact, more ancient than these legends would have you believe. Morgan was a pre-Christian Celtic goddess who was later absorbed into Arthurian myth. Her name literally means Morgan the Fairy. The name *Morgan* probably derives from *mor*, the Welsh word for sea. Celtic mermaids are known as *morgans*, and so *Morgan Le Fey* may also be interpreted as the "Sea Fairy" or the "Mermaid Fairy." Although usually described as a beautiful, dark woman, she is also sometimes envisioned as a mermaid.

Morgan is a master healer, sorceress, and ruler of the Celtic afterlife paradise Avalon, the Isle of Apples. She possesses ancient roots in Italy, too, where she is called Fata Morgana. (*Fata* is Italian for "fairy.") *Fata Morgana* is also the name of a fatal mirage, an optical illusion that lured sailors to their deaths in the Straits of

Messina and for which Morgan is traditionally blamed.

Morgan's first appearance in the Arthurian sagas is in Geoffrey of Monmouth's 12th-century *Life of Merlin*, in which she appears as a benevolent healer. Later versions of Arthurian myth were compiled by Cistercian monks who determined that all Pagan-friendly references in the story must be amended or deleted. Morgan began to be portrayed as the saga's primary villain, a sorceress supreme who commits incest and plots Camelot's downfall. (In the earliest version, she and Arthur have no family kinship.) As attitudes toward witches became increasingly negative, so Morgan was portrayed as increasingly villainous.

In the light of the Neo-Pagan revival, Morgan has been reassessed, most notably in Marion Zimmer Bradley's 1982 novel *The Mists of Avalon*, which re-envisioned her as a heroic Pagan priestess. She is beloved among modern goddess devotees, although she generally retains her villainous reputation in her many appearances in popular culture. She is still usually cast as the villain in fictional depictions of King Arthur. In the *Madame Xanadu* comic book series, Camelot's fall is blamed on Morgan's selfish scheming.

Naamah

The Hebrew name Naamah may be interpreted as "The Charmer," as in a caster of spells, the equivalent of "enchantress." An ancient and mysterious spirit, her first appearance in the Bible occurs in Genesis 4:22, which identifies her as a descendent of Cain and the sister of Tubal Cain, the first ironworker. Other Jewish holy books add details to her legend: the Talmud describes Naamah as a shaman, cymbal player, and singer whose alluring, charming voice lures people to idolatry. According to the Zohar, Kabbalah's Book of Splendor, Naamah is a sea spirit who is "alive to this day."

Naamah may be the woman who fell in love with the rebel angel, Azazel. She may also have had love affairs with King Solomon and Samael, the Poison Angel. She is sometimes considered the mother of the demon Ashmodai, and of the Nephilim, a race of giant, mysterious elder beings. Naamah's primary and most long-lasting relationship seems to be with Lilith, her sometime ally and sometime rival.

Nephthys

Although often overshadowed by her more famous twin sister, Isis, Nephthys is also a powerful spirit of magic and sorcery. Nephthys has dominion over darkness, decay, death, and immortality. She guards the thresholds between life and death, fertility and sterility, oblivion and immortality. Nephthys is the goddess of liminality.

The ancient Egyptians called their country the "Black Land": black, the color of rich, fertile soil, was identified with life, abundance, regeneration, and rejuvenation. Just outside the Black Land loomed the Red Land, the harsh, dry desert that challenged human survival. (The Egyptians considered red an ominous color. They called malevolent magic "red magic," not "black magic.") In Egypt, the dividing line between fertile earth and the desert, the black and the red, was visible. One could literally stand with one foot on fertile land, the other on barren soil. Nephthys rules this liminal borderline.

Her colors are black and red. Her emblem is a skull and crossbones. Creatures most associated with Nephthys include snakes, vultures, and crows. Her planet is the moon. Nephthys is the mother of Anubis, the Egyptian jackal deity who first invented mummification, although she shares custody of him with Isis, his adoptive mother. Nephthys is an ally of Isis and her partner in magical spells and rituals.

Nicnevin

The name of this Scottish witch goddess may be an Anglicized version of the Scots Gaelic, *Nic an Neamhain*, or "Daughter of Frenzy." Nicnevin is among the spirits associated with the raucous, night-riding

Wild Hunt. Nicnevin flies through the night accompanied by flocks of honking geese, her sacred birds. Geese are among those creatures classified as psychopomps: escorts to the realms beyond. Nicnevin is known as the "Bone Mother."

October 31st, Halloween, marks the festival of Samhain, the beginning of the Celtic dark half of the year and a time when the veils between worlds are at their sheerest. Portals open between the realms of the living and the dead. It's also Nicnevin's sacred night; she is traditionally honored with celebratory feasting and toasting. Nicnevin responds to petitions and grants wishes directed toward her on Samhain. Although usually invisible, on Samhain, Nicnevin appears to devotees as she flies through the air, accompanied by an entourage of laughing witches and honking geese. She may manifest as an old hag or as a youthful, beautiful woman. Nicnevin wears a long gray mantle and carries a magic wand. She is a water witch capable of transforming water into rocks and sea into dry land—and vice versa.

Odin

Lord of shamanism, ecstasy, and esoteric wisdom, Odin is the patron of poetry, magic, and the heroic dead. Known as the All-Father, he is a patriarch, an occult master, a restless, wandering wizard, and a formidable trickster. The patron of witches, occultists, and spiritual

The Weiser Field Guide to Witches

seekers, Odin is a magical practitioner and spiritual seeker, too. His thirst and quest for wisdom is endless. Odin willingly traded an eye for one mouthful of water from the Well of Wisdom. Determined to master the runes, Odin pierced himself and then hung for nine days and nights in shamanic ritual on the World Tree. He died a shamanic death in order to be reborn as the rune-master. The Tarot card *The Hanged Man* may depict this ritual, not a literal hanging.

Devotion to Odin once spread across the entire Germanic and Norse world. Other versions of his name include Votan, Woden, and Wotan. Wednesday is his sacred day, literally Woden's Day. He reputedly answers to over 175 different aliases and *noms de guerre*. Odin's familiar ravens, *Hugin* and *Munin*— "Thought" and "Memory"—fly all over Earth each morning, returning with news, gossip, and secrets to whisper in his ear.

Odin travels all over Earth as well as through the sky, riding his magical steed and leading a procession of spirits, ghosts, heroes, and heroines. Their passing is signaled by storms and powerful winds. Post-Christianity, this parade of spirits became known as the Wild Hunt. The Church described it as a parade of the damned, and warned the faithful to keep away lest they be ensnared and forced to join. Odin is the primary Wild Hunter. Sometimes he leads the Wild Hunt alone; sometimes he is accompanied by a female co-leader. Allegedly, if you hear a raven's caw at night, it means that the Wild Hunt—and Odin—draw near.

Odin sometimes wanders Earth in the guise of a shabby, dusty traveler. The clue to his identity tends to be his missing eye, although it is not always easy to spot. He may also travel disguised as a bird. Those who are gracious to him are rewarded. Those who are rude eventually regret their behavior.

Odin continues to be venerated in various Neo-Pagan spiritual traditions like Asatru, as well as by witches. He stars in Richard Wagner's *Ring Cycle* of operas and appears in many works of fiction, including a pivotal role in Neil Gaiman's 2001 novel, *American Gods*.

Ogun

The west African spirit of iron, Ogun is iron. Hold a blade or a horseshoe in your hand, and you hold Ogun.

Ogun is the patron of metal workers, who traditionally also served as shamans, sorcerers, healers, and ritual leaders. By extension, he has become a patron of shamans, fortune-tellers, and witches, too.

Veneration of Ogun is at least as old as the Iron Age, which in Africa began in approximately 500 BC. His worship is not exclusive to one ethnic group, but has spread throughout the region. He is among the very few deities shared by various west African pantheons. Variants of his name include Gu, Gun, Ogoun, and Ogou. He is also venerated by various African Diaspora spiritual traditions, including Candomblé, Santeria, and Vodou. Devotees of Palo may know him under the name Sarabanda or Zarabanda.

West African myths describe how Ogun cut the first paths through Earth's primordial wilderness. He crafted the very first tools for hunting, protection, war, healing, and magic. Ogun epitomizes the solitary forest-dwelling witch-doctor. He knows the magical secrets of metalworking but, living in close proximity with hunters and herbalists, knows their secrets, too. In modern Vodou, he is among the spirits most closely identified with transformational magic and *loups-garoux*.

Ogun is usually envisioned as a powerful, charismatic, very handsome man with radiant, fiery eyes. His sacred animals include snakes and dogs. He is associated with red parrots and parakeets. Ogun rides a beautiful white stallion or a spotted hyena, symbolizing his mastery of witchcraft (with which hyenas are closely associated in Africa).

Oshun

Oshun is the youngest, sweetest, and most beautiful of the spirits known as *orishas*, the ancestral spirits of the Yoruba people who live in what is now modern Nigeria. They are venerated in African Diaspora traditions like Cuba's Santeria and Brazil's Candomblé. Other variant spellings of her name include Ochun and Oxum.

Oshun is a powerful diviner and witch. She removes malevolent spells from her devotees, especially those cast using the power of botanicals. Oshun has dominion over things that flow: fresh water, honey, love, money, and mother's milk, for instance. Her power extends to various parts of the human anatomy, particularly the reproductive organs. She fulfills devotees' wishes, providing wealth, employment, love, beauty, and protection. She rules romance, beauty, prosperity, and magical knowledge.

Oshun appears in various guises. Her most common manifestation is of a gorgeous young woman, usually dressed in shades of gold, orange, or yellow—her sacred colors. She may wear or carry a magic mirror so that she can admire herself whenever she chooses, but also to enable her to scry. Oshun may also appear in the form of a mermaid or a ragged swamp witch, because after all, swamps are fresh water, too.

Oshun's sacred number is five. Her symbols include pumpkins and cowrie shells. Her sacred creatures include vultures, buzzards, parrots, peacocks, alligators, crocodiles, and leopards.

Oya

The spirit of Africa's Niger River, Oya is a master sorceress in possession of great fonts of knowledge. She is also a weather witch with power over storms, winds, and hurricanes. Oya rules the marketplace, which in Yoruba cosmology is considered the magical domain of women. Other names for her include Yansa or Iansa.

In addition to the marketplace, Oya has dominion over the cemetery. She presides over healing and necromantic divination. She is the sacred guardian of spirit mediums. Oya can protect against hauntings and banish ghosts from nightmares, homes, and elsewhere.

Pasiphae

Most famous as the wife of Crete's King Minos and mother of their famous children, Ariadne and the Minotaur, Pasiphae is no mere mortal queen; she's an ancient and powerful Minoan moon goddess with dominion over witchcraft and magic.

Circe and Hekate are Pasiphae's sisters. Medea is her niece. Pasiphae is just as skilled a witch as her sisters. In one myth, she suspects her husband of cheating on her. Pasiphae casts a spell so that he ejaculates poisonous snakes and scorpions, instantly killing any mortal woman with whom he tries to have sex. Only Pasiphae herself or another immortal goddess can survive an encounter with Minos.

Pasiphae can be benevolent, too. Once upon a time, she presided over an oracular shrine in Thalamae, Greece where devotees slept in hopes of receiving prophetic dreams from the goddess. The daughter of Helios the sun, she shared shrines with her father.

Simbi

This Congolese water snake spirit rules all aspects of magic. He protects magical practitioners and offers them his tutelage. He can also bestow clairvoyance and other psychic gifts as well as magical prowess. Simbi is a master healer and botanist. He knows everything there is to know about spirit-derived or magical diseases. In addition to conventional ailments, Simbi can heal illnesses caused by hexes, curses, or disease demons. Among the gifts he bestows on devotees is the power to accurately diagnose. In addition to magic, Simbi has dominion over communications, crossroads, and currents. Because of shared associations with water, snakes, and magic, Simbi is identified with the prophet Moses.

Tezcatlipoca

Aztec divine sorcerer and Lord of the Crossroads, Tezcatlipoca is the patron of witches, shamans, magicians, and diviners—especially mirror gazers. His name means "Smoking Mirror": Tezcatlipoca sees everything in his obsidian mirror, something akin to the *Lord of the Rings'* all-seeing Eye. Tezcatlipoca lives inside Earth's core in a mirrored realm populated by jaguars.

Tezcatlipoca presides over the ancient magical art of *nahualism*: complex, intense, intertwined soul relationships between people and their animal allies. Nahualism involves magical transformations and Tezcatlipoca, master shaman and shape-shifter, can take many forms. His favored forms include a coyote, jaguar, monkey, owl, skunk, or man. A clue to his true identity: he may be missing one foot, or he may limp. His favorite time to appear is midnight.

Tezcatlipoca is now most famous as the rival of his brother Quetzalcoatl, the Plumed Serpent, whose fall from grace was orchestrated by Tezcatlipoca's smoke and mirrors. When Christian missionaries arrived in Mexico, they perceived the tragic, suffering Quetzalcoatl as a Christ-figure and identified his rival, the unrepentant sorcerer Tezcatlipoca, as the devil. Consequently, Tezcatlipoca is frequently portrayed as an evil villain in children's mythology books and popular media, but that's an over-simplification. He is an extremely complex spirit, both a destroyer and a creator.

Thoth

Thoth is so primeval that he existed before time. In some Egyptian creation myths, Thoth is the supreme creator who created himself by speaking his own name. Even in myths in which he is not the supreme creator, Thoth does his fair share of creating. Egyptian myth credits Thoth with the invention of writing, gambling, magic spells, star-gazing, engineering, geometry, botany, medicine, and mathematics. He was the first alchemist and the author of the very first book on the topic, *The Book of Thoth*, a collection of magic spells and rituals so powerful that it was eventually locked up and hidden away.

The name *Thoth* is based on the Greek pronunciation of the Egyptian word *Tehuti*, which is related to Egyptian words for moon, measure, ibis and crystal. In his guise as Patron of Scribes, Thoth bears the head of an ibis; as a master magician, he manifests as a baboon. Although these are his most common forms, Thoth can appear in any form that he desires.

Thoth tutored Isis, teaching her everything he knew. She may be the only one who surpasses his magical knowledge, but even Isis still needs his magical help sometimes.

The Weiser Field Guide to Witches

This Aztec spirit of magic, healing, love, sex, desire, cleansing, filth, and garbage is the matron guardian goddess of witches, female healers, and midwives. (Her name is pronounced *tla-zohl-tee-oh-tul*.) Tlazolteotl cleanses Earth and individuals of sin, shame, and spiritual debris, and is credited with inventing the *temescal*, also spelled *temazcal* or *temazcalli*, the Aztec sweat bathhouse used not only for physical cleansing but also for spiritual and magical purification rites.

When Spanish conquistadors first arrived in Mexico, they found much that was unfamiliar to shock them, but what shocked them most about Tlazolteotl was her very familiarity. Tlazolteotl is traditionally depicted riding on a broomstick, dressed in nothing but a peaked bark hat. Owls, bats, and ravens accompany her. The conquistadors and their accompanying priests took one look at her image and recognized Tlazolteotl as a witch. (Another votive image of Tlazolteotl, which depicts her in the guise of a naked, squatting woman grimacing in childbirth, is now more famous as it appears as the stolen idol in the hit movie *Raiders of the Lost Ark*.) Veneration of Tlazolteotl was outlawed but never completely suppressed, and she remains a popular Neo-Pagan goddess.

Tubal Cain

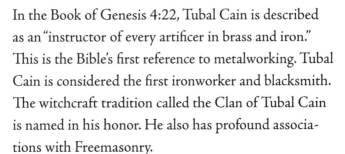

In the Book of Genesis 4:22, Tubal Cain is described as an "instructor of every artificer in brass and iron." This is the Bible's first reference to metalworking. Tubal Cain is considered the first ironworker and blacksmith. The witchcraft tradition called the Clan of Tubal Cain is named in his honor. He also has profound associations with Freemasonry.

Tubal Cain has interesting relatives. He is a seventh-generation descendent of Cain, the first murderer and outcast. Tubal Cain's father is Lamekh and his mother is Zillah, whose name means "shadow." Witch goddess Naamah is Tubal Cain's sister.

There are different versions of Tubal Cain's fate. In one, Tubal Cain is murdered by his father; according to other versions, Tubal Cain survived the great deluge, not by catching a ride on Noah's ark but by hiding deep within mines. According to this version, Tubal Cain still walks the Earth.

Yemaya

Sacred Queen of the Sea, beautiful Yemaya rules anything pertaining to women. Among the most powerful, beloved, and magical of the Yoruba spirits known as orishas, Yemaya's associations with the ocean are profound. She resides *in* the sea, she is the spirit *of* the sea, and Yemaya *is* the sea. Her nature resembles the ocean: beautiful, sensuous, filled with treasure and abundance, but also tempestuous and dangerous.

Yemaya may manifest in the guise of a woman, a mermaid, or any denizen of the deep. Among her manifestations is a witch who dwells in mangrove swamps and wooded lagoons. Witchy Yemaya is closely allied with Ogun. She is the protective guardian of witches and occultists.

Yemaya's number is seven, as in the seven seas. Her metal is silver and she is associated with the moon and the night stars. Her colors are clear crystal and different shades of blue. In her witchy aspect, she is closely identified with indigo.

CHAPTER 6

Entertaining Witches

Imagine our most ancient ancestors, back in some primordial era, sitting outside after dark, attempting to entertain each other by telling suspenseful stories. Who starred in those old tales? We don't have to have been there to know: witches did.

Now fast-forward to the 21st century, where kids sit in rooms filled with the most modern technology, entertaining themselves with video games or DVDs. Who stars in these new forms of entertainment? Witches do.

For as long as people have enjoyed being entertained, witches have served as inspiration—and continue to do so at an ever-increasing rate. Witches star in ancient myths, fairy tales, and folktales from literally every culture. They feature in Elizabethan plays, Victorian novels, Pre-Raphaelite paintings, television comedies, gory horror movies, and entertainment intended for small children.

Witches have *always* served as a creative muse for artists in one way or another, although *how* witches and their craft are portrayed depends upon era, culture, and an individual artist's inclinations. While witches have inspired art and entertainment, in turn art and entertainment have influenced how witches are perceived and understood, whether favorably or not.

Witches have inspired literally countless works, and thousands of pages could be devoted to these "entertaining witches" alone. What follows is just a random sampling of some of the more significant and popular witches to have entertained, amused, thrilled, and chilled us. Because these witches were created to entertain, many are figures of fantasy, or at least partially so.

Famous Witches of Literature

There's nothing like a good witch story to keep people entertained. Witches feature in literature of all kinds, from classical to Gothic to pulp fiction to fantasy to reality-based historic novels. There are thousands of books in the English language alone that feature witches. One can read about virtually any kind of witch one desires: evil witches, sexy witches, heroic witches, scheming witches, incompetent witches, savior witches, ugly old witches, cute little witches . . . the variety is endless.

Witches appear in the earliest surviving examples of literature: Euripides' Greek tragedy *Medea*, first produced in 431 BC, for instance. *The Golden Ass*, the late 2nd-century AD novel by Lucius Apuleius and the only Latin novel to survive in its entirety, features several witches. Fictional depictions of witches continue to be immensely popular, although how witches are portrayed has changed dramatically over the years.

A very interesting phenomenon has been the rise, at the very tail end of the 20th century, of the witch as a sympathetic character, especially in literature intended for children and young adults. Once upon a time, with very few exceptions, witches in literature were intended as villains or horror motifs. The most sympathetic witches in literature were usually not really witches at all: a common theme features a woman in mortal danger after she has been falsely accused of being a witch.

Even into the later years of the 20th century, witches were perceived as disreputable and certainly not considered good role models. The phenomenal success of the *Harry Potter* series of novels changed this perception, at least in literature. In the post-*Harry Potter* world, children's books are filled with witches who are as likely to be benevolent or humorous as they are to be scary and malevolent.

Celestina

A witch is the star and title character of *La Celestina*, a Spanish literary classic that is considered the first true novel to appear in the West. Since its publication in 1491, it has been translated into English, French, German, and Italian. *La Celestina* was first published anonymously, and for good reason. The book, which initially appeared at the height of the Spanish Inquisition, expresses empathy for witches, prostitutes, and poor struggling women in general. The author, now believed to be Fernando Rojas, was aware of the dangers facing witches. Fear of persecution is mentioned in the story. Celestina herself was once punished by being placed in the torture device known as the stocks.

Celestina is a knowledgeable spell-caster, midwife, perfumer, herbalist, healer, procuress, and professional go-between. In short, she does whatever she can to earn a living. Her specialty is renewing female virginity via some sophisticated sewing techniques. Celestina and the prostitutes in her employ are smart, hardworking, and down-to-earth, as opposed to the narcissistic, selfish gentry featured in the novel.

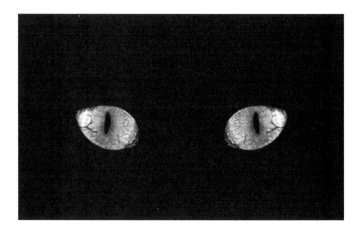

Dorrie
the Witch

The subject of a series of beloved children's books, Dorrie the little witch lives in Witchville with her mother, the Big Witch, her faithful black cat, Gink, and another witch, Cook. Dorrie's hat is always on crooked and her socks never match. Dorrie has a talent for finding trouble, but she always manages to save the day, emerging as a humble heroine. Her adventures include outwitting goblins, rescuing Witchville's Book of Shadows, and protecting the witches of Witchville from the nightmare-inducing Dreamyard monsters.

Written and illustrated by Patricia Coombs (born July 23, 1926), the *Dorrie* series consists of twenty books. The first book in the series, *Dorrie's Magic*, was published in 1962; the twentieth, *Dorrie and the Haunted Schoolhouse*, appeared thirty years later in 1992.

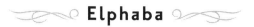

Elphaba

Wicked: The Life and Times of the Wicked Witch of the West, the 1995 bestselling novel by Gregory Maguire, draws its inspiration from both L. Frank Baum's *Wizard of Oz* series of books and the 1939 MGM movie musical based on them. *Wicked* considers the question: *why* is the Wicked Witch of the West considered wicked?

Prior to *Wicked*, the Wicked Witch was nameless, although one subsequently unused movie script called her Gulcheria. Maguire named her Elphaba, deriving the name from L. Frank Baum's initials. The story follows her life, beginning at conception. Elphaba's strict religious fundamentalist father considers her green skin to be punishment for her mother's sins. Elphaba attends college in the Emerald City, where her roommate is the beautiful but shallow Galinda, the future Glinda the Good Witch. Elphaba is a sensitive crusader for justice and an animal rights activist who becomes involved in the underground resistance to the wizard's oppressive regime and is thus branded a wicked enemy of the state.

Grand High Witch

The Grand High Witch of All the World rules witches in Roald Dahl's 1983 children's novel, *The Witches*. Her function is to supervise witches' predations on children. She is so all-powerful and terrible that even the other witches fear her.

According to *The Witches*, each nation on Earth hosts a secret society of witches. Witches residing in every country—Norway, England, and so forth—attend an annual secret convention which features a lecture by the Grand High Witch, who travels the globe, attending these conventions. The main character of *The Witches* is a little boy who accidentally stumbles into a witch convention and is transformed into a mouse by the Grand High Witch. With the help of his wise, witch-hunting grandmother, he must rescue the other children of the world from sharing his fate.

Although this is clearly fantasy, an author's note at the beginning of *The Witches* advises readers that the story "is not a fairy-tale. It is about REAL WITCHES." Real witches, writes Dahl "*. . . are not actually human beings at all . . . They are demons in human shape.*" A "real witch," he continues, "hates children with a red-hot passion and spends all her time plotting to get rid of the children in her home territory."

The book serves as a children's witch-hunting manual, offering instructions for recognizing witches.

In this fantasy universe, witches are *always* female. (To be fair, the book points out that ghouls are male—but not as harmful as witches.)

Real witches are invariably bald, and must wear wigs to conceal this fact. They have exceptionally large nostrils enabling them to better smell and detect children, their primary prey. The cleaner the child, the easier it is for witches to smell them. Witches always wear gloves when out in public, because they lack human fingernails—they have cat-like claws instead. Like the goblins in George MacDonald's 1872 fantasy novel, *The Princess and the Goblin*, witches have no toes, which makes wearing shoes very uncomfortable.

The Witches received the Whitbread Award and the Federation of Children's Books Group Award in the UK in 1983. Anjelica Huston plays the Grand High Witch in the 1990 movie adaptation of *The Witches*, directed by Nicholas Roeg.

Harry Potter

The most famous magical practitioner in the world, fictional or otherwise, Harry Potter stars in a series of novels written by J. K. Rowling and named in his honor. Books in the series include *Harry Potter and the Sorcerer's Stone* (1997); *Harry Potter and the Chamber of Secrets* (1998); *Harry Potter and the Prisoner of Azkaban* (1999); *Harry Potter and the Goblet of Fire* (2000); *Harry Potter and the Order of the Phoenix* (2003); *Harry Potter and the Half-Blood Prince* (2005); and *Harry Potter and the Deathly Hallows* (2007).

To describe *Harry Potter* as an international literary phenomenon is a grave understatement. Hundreds of millions of books have been sold. Extraordinary security measures were taken to prevent plots from being leaked before each of the later books was published. The series has been translated into many languages. Spin-offs include movies, video games, toys, and clothing.

Harry Potter has also had an impact on the history of witches. In the wake of its incredible financial success, witches now routinely appear as heroes in entertainment geared toward children, a trend that was not common before.

The vast majority of characters in the series are witches and wizards. (In the *Harry Potter* universe, witches are exclusively female. Their male counterparts are wizards.) Thus they are the heroes, heroines, villains and supporting characters. Witches in the *Harry Potter* universe are complex individuals with nuanced goals, relationships, and personalities.

Harry spends his first eleven years in misery, living with the Dursleys, his abusive relatives. On his eleventh birthday, he unexpectedly receives an invitation to attend the Hogwarts School of Witchcraft and Wizardry, and his life is transformed. Harry is revealed to be a wizard, and he enters a parallel word where witches and wizards reside. The mysteries of his childhood and his parents' deaths are revealed. The novels follow Harry's adventures as he battles his nemesis, the evil wizard Lord Voldemort.

Harry is brave, idealistic, and fiercely loyal to those he loves. Although unquestionably the hero to readers, many characters in the novels view him with suspicion, wondering whether he is truly a good wizard or a bad one. Actor Daniel Radcliffe portrays the young wizard in the *Harry Potter* movie series.

Hermione Granger

Harry Potter's best friend in the *Harry Potter* series of novels, Hermione Granger is a central figure and heroine in each of the seven books. Hermione meets Harry when they both arrive at Hogwarts School of Witchcraft and Wizardry. She is a muggle-born witch, meaning that she does not come from a lineage of witches. This causes some of the denizens of the wizarding universe to treat her disrespectfully. Ironically, she ranks among the most skilled and talented of all magical practitioners.

Hermione is extremely studious and hard-working, consistently reproaching Harry and other Hogwarts students for shirking their studies. For this reason, when the first *Harry Potter* novel was published, parents and educators embraced Hermione as a role model for children—highly unusual for a witch character. In the *Harry Potter* movies, Hermione Granger is portrayed by actress Emma Watson.

Jadis the White Witch

The *Chronicles of Narnia*, a series of seven novels written by author C. S. Lewis, may be enjoyed purely as children's fantasy, but they may also be understood as a Christian metaphor. Thus it is not surprising that a witch is cast in the role of the villain.

Jadis the White Witch appears in two volumes of *The Chronicles of Narnia*. She appears in *The Lion, the Witch and the Wardrobe* (1950), the first book in the series to be published. Four children are evacuated from London during World War II air raids and sent to live in a mysterious old professor's country home. While exploring the house, the children climb into a large wardrobe, where they discover a portal to another realm: Narnia. Jadis has cast a spell over Narnia so that it is perpetually winter. She also appears in another novel in the series, *The Magician's Nephew* (1955), a prequel that explains how Narnia fell under her spell.

Jadis, a proverbial wicked witch, demonstrates terrific vitality and is an extremely fun character, particularly when she, too, passes through a portal and wreaks havoc in London. In the 2005 film version of *The Lion, the Witch and the Wardrobe*, the White Witch is portrayed by Tilda Swinton.

Lois Barclay

The heroine of *Lois the Witch*, an 1861 novella by the popular Victorian author Elizabeth Gaskell, is an English minister's daughter who is orphaned and forced for economic reasons to leave England and the man she loves. Lois seeks refuge with relatives she has never met in Salem Village. She arrives in 1692, just in time for Salem's witch panic.

Lois is kind, responsible, and sensitive, and she does her best to ingratiate herself with her long-lost relatives—but to little avail. They are greedy, dour fundamentalists and, as portrayed by Gaskell, possibly suffering from mental illness. Lois' innocent reminiscences of English village Halloween customs contribute to placing her life in danger.

Despite the book's title, Lois is not a witch. The sole possible witch in the novel is a female Indian servant, probably intended to evoke memories of the historic accused Salem witch, Tituba. The author's intent was to demonstrate how innocent women were ensnared in the injustices of witch hunting.

Serafina Pekkala

His Dark Materials is a trilogy of novels written by Philip Pullman. Novels in this series include *The Golden Compass* (US title)/*Northern Lights* (UK title) (1995); *The Subtle Knife* (1997); and *The Amber Spyglass* (2000). The novels chronicle the adventures of young heroine Lyra Bellacqua and her friends as they navigate a dangerous landscape populated by witches, angels, ghosts, talking armored bears, and other wonders. Serafina Pekkala is the witch queen of this realm.

The witches in this universe are exclusively female, although served and loved by men. Their female children inherit their mother's magical power and become witches, too, while male children are sent to live with their fathers. The witches are fierce, beautiful, righteous heroines who provide safety for children rather than trying to eat or harm them. Serafina is among the novels' primary heroines. Actress Eva Green portrayed Serafina in the 2007 film adaptation of *The Golden Compass*.

The Weird Sisters

Among the most famous and influential literary witches of all time, the Weird Sisters star in William Shakespeare's 17th-century tragedy, *Macbeth*. *Macbeth* was composed in approximately 1605 as an attempt by the playwright to gain the good graces of James I, England's new king. James was known to be immensely fascinated and terrified by witches, whom he believed had made an attempt on his life, and so Shakespeare wrote a play in which witches figure prominently. *Macbeth* remains among Shakespeare's most popular plays and is constantly in production.

Macbeth's witches are known as the Weird Sisters. Although the witches may indeed appear strange, the term "weird" actually derives from Anglo-Saxon myth.

The original, pre-Shakespearian Weird Sisters are a trio of goddesses of destiny similar to the Fates or Norns. It is unclear whether *Macbeth*'s witches only foretell the future or whether they cause it.

No need to wait for *Macbeth*'s witches: they appear in the first scene, beginning the play with their words, "When shall we three meet again . . ." The Weird Sisters are not subtle. They are very obviously witches. They are shown brewing what they describe as a "hell broth" in a cauldron of spooky ingredients. They invoke Hekate as their goddess and conjure up apparitions as Macbeth requests. Numerous filmed versions of *Macbeth* exist, including many different interpretations of the Weird Sisters.

The Weird Sisters are allegedly responsible for a real-life curse popularly believed to afflict productions of *Macbeth*. A theatrical superstition advises that it is dangerously unlucky to utter the real name of this play inside a theater, and so it is typically called "The Scottish Play." Different legends explain the origins of the curse: Shakespeare may have borrowed some of the play's spells from real witches who were then disgruntled not to be credited (or paid). Alternatively, a prop-master may have stolen the cauldron used in the initial production from real witches, who then placed a curse on their missing tool. Another version suggests that the danger afflicting productions of *Macbeth* is not technically a curse, but real witches. Allegedly uttering the name "Macbeth" serves to summon the ghosts of angry, offended witches who then proceed to cause mayhem and harm. The curse allegedly first manifested at the play's premier performance, at which an actor died when a real dagger was substituted for a prop.

Famous Witches of the Movies

For as long as there have been movies, witches have cast their spell over them, appearing in some of the earliest films. French director Georges Méliès (1861–1938) is among the pioneering first fathers of cinema. In his *The Sorcerer, the Prince and the Good Fairy*, made in 1900, nine witches turn a handsome prince into an old tramp. The name of his 1901 film *Chez le Sorcière* (The Witch's House) explicitly describes its setting.

Witches and women accused of being witches star in Hollywood silent movies like *The Witch of Salem*

(1913) or *Witchcraft* (1916). The 1922 Swedish film *Häxan*, although intended as titillating entertainment, portrays historic details of witch trials with remarkable accuracy. Among its themes is the sexual victimization and abuse of women during the witch hunting era.

Witches appear in movies from around the world and in every cinematic genre: summer blockbusters, horror movies, romantic comedies, films intended for small children, grindhouse, art house, and more. Audiences never seem to tire of watching movie witches. Among the thousands of films featuring witches are Tim Burton's *Sleepy Hollow*; *Eye of the Devil* starring Sharon Tate; *Drag Me To Hell*; Italian horror classic *Black Sunday*; Mexican horror classic *The Witch's*

Mirror; *Suspiria*; *Bedknobs and Broomsticks*; *Hocus Pocus*; Ingmar Bergman's *The Seventh Seal*; *The Blair Witch Project*; *Burn, Witch, Burn*; *The Burning Times*; *The Conqueror Worm*; *The Lord of the Rings*; *The Craft*; *The Witches*; *The Witches of Eastwick*; numerous filmed versions of Shakespeare's *Macbeth*; assorted animated Disney films; and the *Harry Potter* film series.

What follows is a guide to some of the most famous and popular movie witches.

Bellatrix Lestrange

As portrayed by Helena Bonham Carter, Bellatrix Lestrange appears in several films in the *Harry Potter* series: *Harry Potter and the Goblet of Fire, Harry Potter and the Order of the Phoenix,* and *Harry Potter and the Half-Blood Prince.* (She is also scheduled to appear in the as-yet unreleased—at time of this book's publication—two-part film, *Harry Potter and the Deathly Hallows.*)

In a movie universe where virtually every character is a witch or wizard, hero, heroine, and villain alike, Bellatrix is the one who corresponds to the archetype of the wicked witch. Unlike virtually every other witch in this series, Bellatrix dresses exclusively in black and has wild, disheveled hair. She terrorizes Harry in the manner that the Wicked Witch of the West terrorizes Dorothy in *The Wizard of Oz.*

Bellatrix is fanatically devoted to Lord Voldemort, the Dark Lord whose name must not be spoken. The most loyal of his devotees, Bellatrix is a formidable witch, second in power only to Voldemort. Her relationship with Voldemort, which ultimately leads to her doom, corresponds to the medieval witch hunter's conception of a witch's relationship with the devil. (The reticence shown by most characters to utter Voldemort's name recalls the old saying, "Speak not the devil's name, lest he come.")

Gillian Holroyd

Kim Novak portrays Gillian Holroyd in the 1958 movie *Bell, Book and Candle*. Gillian is a glamorous, storm-raising Greenwich Village witch in the days when that downtown New York City neighborhood was the epicenter of bohemian life. Gillian is beautiful, blonde, and incredibly stylish with a chic, expensive wardrobe. (*Bell, Book and Candle* earned an Academy Award nomination for costume design.)

Although suffering from ennui and weary of witch-craft, Gillian is the most powerful of the film's many witches, including her aunt Queenie, played by Elsa Lanchester, the original Bride of Frankenstein. Gillian's bongo-playing brother Nicky is portrayed by a young Jack Lemmon. The movie's true star may be Pyewacket, Gillian's Siamese cat familiar. When Gillian demands that Pyewacket fetch her a lover, specifically her new upstairs neighbor, played by Jimmy Stewart, the cat delivers.

The movie's title refers to Roman Catholic rites of exorcism, which do not figure into the plot. Apparently some considered this title too oblique. When released in Italy, *Bell, Book and Candle* was called *Una Strega in Paradiso* (A Witch in Paradise).

Glinda the Good Witch

Glinda emerges from a floating bubble, dressed in pink and wearing a high crown and wings. When she identifies herself as a witch, Dorothy, *The Wizard of Oz*'s heroine, is taken aback: she hadn't realized that witches could be beautiful. As played by Billie Burke, Glinda corresponds visually to the stereotype of a fairy queen, and so it's natural that people sometimes forget that there are *two* witches in the 1939 MGM musical *The Wizard of Oz* (in addition to the one crushed by Dorothy Gale's house).

Upon first meeting, Glinda asks Dorothy the enduring question, "Are you a good witch or a bad one?" Apparently in the world of Oz one cannot be both. Ironically, although Glinda *looks* beautiful and is self-identified as a "good witch," she's not always very nice. Glinda teases the Wicked Witch with the ruby slippers, but then slips the shoes onto Dorothy's feet. She neglects to tell Dorothy that the ruby slippers can magically carry her home until after Dorothy has killed the Wicked Witch.

Glinda, like the Wicked Witch, has transcended her movie role to become an international icon. Her image appears on lunchboxes, assorted tchotchkes, t-shirts, and toys, although not to the same extent as the Wicked Witch.

Ina

The beautiful forest witch in the 1956 French film *La Sorcière (The Sorceress)*, Ina has genuine magical powers. As portrayed by Russian actress Marina Vlady, she can heal with her touch and possesses the gift of telekinesis. She cavorts with deer and squirrels.

Ina is a hereditary witch who lives near a swamp in a remote region of Sweden with her grandmother, who warns her away from the fundamentalist villagers who live beyond the woods. The villagers believe that Ina and her family are the literal progeny of the devil. Ina's beauty and innocence draw the attention of a highly educated and rational French engineer, newly arrived in the region to supervise the building of a road. He scoffs at the possibility that Ina might really be a witch—or that witches even exist—and discredits the villagers' deeply held beliefs. His desire to lure Ina from the forest and integrate her into society leads to tragic consequences.

Jennifer

As portrayed by Veronica Lake in the 1942 romantic comedy *I Married a Witch*, Jennifer is a beautiful, sexy, charming witch with a hearty appetite for food, fun, trouble, and romance. Its French director, René Clair, spent the World War II years in the United States. A renowned surrealist, he created a film with what were then magical special effects about a Salem witch and her old sorcerer dad.

Witches in *I Married a Witch* resemble humans, if they choose, but they are another species and can assume various forms. Magic rituals may be used to contain these witches against their will, but they are never actually destroyed. Having spent 270 years imprisoned within a tree, the newly escaped Jennifer is hungry for revenge but her plans backfire and go comically awry.

Although she looks extremely youthful, Jennifer's age is unknown. It is unclear whether she has existed since the days of Pompeii or whether she is only 290 years old. Unlike other movie and television witches, Jennifer does not regret being a witch, nor does she hesitate to use her powers. Jennifer is self-confident, determined, and happy with herself. *I Married a Witch* ends with the strong visual suggestion that this lineage of hereditary witches hasn't ended just because Jennifer married a mortal.

Maleficent

The wicked witch in Walt Disney's 1959 animated feature film, *Sleeping Beauty*, Maleficent is among the most popular of Disney's many beloved villains. A scene stealer, she lights up the screen. Although initially introduced as a "bad fairy," Maleficent quickly transforms into an "evil witch." Her name is the clue to her witch identity. Maleficent derives from *maleficia*, a

Latin word referring to the practice of negative—and typically fatal—witchcraft. The word may be obscure now, but it was once extremely common witch hunter's lingo. Variations on that word appear in the titles of witch hunters' manuals, most notably the *Malleus Maleficarum* or *The Hammer of Witches*, for years a European best-seller second only to the Bible in popularity.

Maleficent is a regal, intimidating, goddess-like witch. She wears a black and red cape, colors traditionally associated with witches. Ravens serve as her familiars. When angered, Maleficent transforms into a bat-winged dragon.

Minnie Castevet

Veteran actress Ruth Gordon portrayed Minnie Castevet, the elderly but vivacious Upper West Side New York City witch in director Roman Polanski's 1968 film, *Rosemary's Baby*. Her husband Roman Castevet, also a witch, is played by Sidney Blackmer.

Although the movie, a huge box office success, is famous now, those unfamiliar with the plot might not immediately realize that Minnie and Roman are witches. The plot hinges on how long it takes their victim, Rosemary, to recognize that the Castevets, her next-door neighbors, are more than just an eccentric older couple. They lack the stereotypical, tell-tale clues that would identify them as witches: no pointy hats, no black cats, no flying broomsticks. The closest thing to a "telltale sign of witchcraft" is Minnie's knowledge of herbs and her production of homemade healing potions.

Minnie and the other witches in *Rosemary's Baby* correspond to the deepest fears of medieval witch hunters—and apparently many modern movie-goers, too. They hide in plain sight, living right next door and blending in perfectly. *Rosemary's Baby* is based on author Ira Levin's 1967 bestselling novel of the same name. Ruth Gordon won the Oscar and Golden Globe awards for best supporting actress for this role, becoming the first person to win an Oscar for portraying a witch.

The Owens Witches

The Owens Witches are a family of hereditary witches in the 1998 American film *Practical Magic*, directed by Griffin Dunne and based on Alice Hoffman's 1995 novel of the same name. Two witch sisters, Frances and Jet Owens (played by Stockard Channing and Dianne Wiest) raise their orphaned nieces, another pair of sisters, Gillian and Sally (played by Nicole Kidman and Sandra Bullock). All beautiful, accomplished, magical women, they are tragically afflicted by the "Owens Curse," which stems from their ancestress, a Salem witch who was condemned by a "hanging committee" of

local women who believed she'd slept with all their husbands. (Historically, no such hanging committee ever
existed. Women were not involved as decision-makers
in colonial Salem, during the witch-trials or any other
legal process.) The curse was ostensibly laid upon the
town, but in practice affects her descendants, as men
who fall in love with Owens women are doomed to die
untimely deaths.

The witches of *Practical Magic* are wild, fun, and
defiant—especially the older generation. They serve
chocolate cake for breakfast and encourage their young
wards to do spellwork instead of homework. The
younger generation suffers more angst. Sally Owens
sells herbal products and possesses valuable powers of
healing. The film attempts to integrate modern Wicca
or Neo-Paganism into fantasies about witches.

Tia Dalma

As portrayed by actress Naomie Harris, Tia Dalma
appears in two installments of the tremendously
popular *Pirates of the Caribbean* series. She appears in
the second film, *Pirates of the Caribbean: Dead Man's
Chest* (2006). The plot of the third movie, *Pirates of the
Caribbean: At World's End* (2007), revolves around the
discovery of her true identity.

Tia is a mysterious character, a fortune-teller
and swamp witch with power over the elements. She
provides other characters with valuable magical tools,

and corresponds to the mythic archetype of the great goddess now demoted to the lowly status of a witch.

Ursula, the Sea Witch

The villain of Disney's 1989 animated feature film *The Little Mermaid* is a conniving octopus-woman who dwells in the grotto where she has been banished. Once upon a time, Ursula was a ruler of the sea, and the plot hinges on her desire to return to power and wreak revenge on those who have supplanted her. She possesses the accoutrements of a traditional witch: a magic mirror, crystal ball, magic potions, and two eel familiars, Flotsam and Jetsam, who resemble sea snakes and venture out to do her bidding. Pat Carroll voiced Ursula's character.

The Wicked Witch of the West

Intended as the villain of the 1939 MGM musical *The Wizard of Oz*, the Wicked Witch of the West has in recent years evolved into a heroine. People are often amazed to realize that she is only onscreen for a total of twelve minutes, as her presence in the movie is so pervasive.

The green-skinned Wicked Witch of the West terrorizes the movie's central character, Dorothy, who has accidentally killed the witch's sister, the Wicked Witch of the East. Dorothy has been given the dead witch's magical ruby red shoes, and the Wicked Witch of the West wants them back.

The film's producers originally sought to cast Gale Sondergaard in the role of the Wicked Witch of the West. Sondergaard's specialty was playing icy, glamorous, beautiful villains. However, too many people objected, insisting that witches must be ugly, and Margaret Hamilton was cast instead. Initially Hamilton was merely intended to look disheveled, but as filming progressed, her appearance was adjusted to make her appear terrifying and grotesque. By the time *The Wizard of Oz* was screened, producers feared they had been too successful. Children at early screenings ran screaming from theaters in terror.

The Wicked Witch of the West flies her broomstick through the air and commands a private army of winged monkeys. She is shown to be an effective crystal gazer, and is capable of throwing fire balls by hand and casting long-distance spells.

The Wicked Witch of the West has emerged as a true cultural icon, transcending her status in the movie. Her image is now found on clothing, lunch boxes, salt and pepper shakers, and jewelry. Hallmark sells Wicked Witch of the West ornaments, and Mattel produces Wicked Witch of the West Barbie dolls.

Yubaba

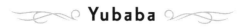

A witch named Yubaba manages the bathhouse of the spirits that is the central stage for Japanese director Hayao Miyazaki's 2001 animated feature film, *Spirited Away*. The film earned Miyazaki an Oscar for animation and shared the prize for best film at the Berlin Film Festival.

Spirited Away presents the adventures of a ten-year-old girl, Chihiro, who is first observed moving to a new home with her parents. En route to the new house, they wander into a mysterious abandoned ghost town. What appears to be an empty landscape is really a resort town for spirits centering on *Abura-ya*, the Bathhouse of the Spirits. Spirits journey from all over to visit, take baths, socialize, rest, and rejuvenate.

Yubaba, whose name recalls Russian fairy-tale witch Baba Yaga, resembles an elderly, elegant central European lady, although she does flaunt a stereotypical witch's large wart. Sharp-tongued, hard-hearted, acquisitive, and greedy, she can transform into a bird and fly. The plot hinges on her rivalry with a sister-witch.

Suzanne Pleshette voices Yubaba in the English language version of *Spirited Away*.

Famous Witches of Sequential Art: Comics and Manga

Sequential art is an art-form in which multiple sequential images are arranged to form a narrative or tell a story and which usually, but not necessarily, incorporates written text. Prehistoric cave art is sometimes considered the most ancient form of sequential art. The most popular modern forms are comic books and manga.

The modern concept of superheroes derives from comic books. Occult practitioners, like Mandrake the Magician, were among the very first superheroes. After all, who else has supernatural powers, if not a witch? There are thousands of witches featured in sequential art. What follow are but some of the most popular and prominent.

Dr. Strange

Stephen Strange was a brilliant surgeon, but he was also egotistical, narcissistic, and an alcoholic. Hitting the bottle too hard one night, he crashed his car, killing his pregnant wife and damaging his hands so badly that he could no longer practice surgery. For a while he hit the skids, but eventually, seeking spiritual solace, Dr.

Strange traveled to Tibet, where he became the acolyte of a cave-dwelling lama known as the Ancient One. After intensive study of sorcery and magic, Dr. Strange emerged as the Master of the Mystical Arts and a very popular superhero.

Dr. Strange made his first appearance in the Marvel Comics universe in 1961, and has since starred in several films, both live-action and animated. According to Marvel Comics mythology, Dr. Strange lives in a Greenwich Village townhouse on Bleecker Street with his wife, the sorceress Clea, and his man-servant and friend, Wong. The house is protected by a magical force field that provides an illusion of invisibility whenever Dr. Strange desires. In 1988 he was promoted to Sorcerer Supreme, although he has now ceded this last title to a younger magical practitioner, Brother Voodoo, now promoted to Doctor Voodoo.

John Constantine

A master sorcerer, John Constantine stars in the Vertigo Comics series *Hellblazer*, although he also makes guest appearances in other Vertigo and DC Comics series including *Swamp Thing*, *The Sandman*, and *Books of Magic*. Constantine and Zatanna were once romantically involved. Unlike many other comic book witches, Constantine has no superpowers. The powers he manifests derive from magical skill and knowledge. He is a hereditary witch from a long line of occult practitioners. One of his ancestors appears as a character in Neil Gaiman's comic series *The Sandman*. Constantine casts spells, creates sigils, conducts séances and is an accomplished exorcist.

Lady Death

Once named Hope, Lady Death is the daughter of a corrupt nobleman in medieval Sweden. Unbeknownst to her, her father is also a sorcerer, in thrall to Lucifer. When local peasants violently rebel, her father escapes, but Hope is captured and falsely accused of being a witch. Tied to a stake and about to be set aflame, Hope desperately recalls one of her father's incantations. It summons a demon who offers her a classic bargain: he will rescue her if she renounces her soul and agrees to serve the infernal powers. Hope agrees, and is instantly transported to Hell, where she eventually transforms into the anti-heroine, Lady Death. After many battles and obstacles, Lady Death emerges as Hell's new ruler.

Madame Xanadu

"Enter freely and be unafraid," reads the sign on Madame Xanadu's Greenwich Village fortune-telling parlor. Madame Xanadu fits the archetype of a dethroned goddess forced to labor as a witch. Once upon a time, she was Nimue, a goddess in King Arthur's

Britain and sister of Morgan Le Fay. In an attempt to save Camelot from doom, Nimue cast a spell over her lover, Merlin, but in the process lost her own goddess powers, although still retaining her formidable magical knowledge.

Nimue wandered through the centuries, finally receiving her new name—Madame Xanadu—at the court of Kublai Khan. Because she is *almost* immortal, Madame Xanadu has had encounters with many interesting historic characters, including Marie Antoinette and Jack the Ripper. She now lives in Greenwich Village, not far from the home of Dr. Strange. Madame Xanadu first appeared in DC Comics in 1978. Her own Vertigo Comics series debuted in 2008. Madame Xanadu is portrayed casting spells, crafting runes, reading cards, and concocting powerful potions.

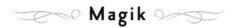

Magik

Like her brother, the X-Man Colossus, Magik was born in Russia. Her birth name is Illyana Rasputina. If that name seems familiar, it's because it's intended to invoke the historic Rasputin, the Russian monk and advisor to the last tsar. Some believe Rasputin to have been a sorcerer. Magik, like Rasputin, is an ambiguous but very powerful character.

Kidnapped as a child and transported to a hell dimension known as Limbo, Illyana accrued magical knowledge while simultaneously developing her own mutant powers of teleportation, transforming into the powerful sorceress known as Magik. She first appeared in the Marvel Comics universe in 1975, but has become increasingly popular. She is now a member of the hero team the New Mutants, and was long rumored to be in the running to replace Dr. Strange as Sorcerer Supreme (though that title has now been given to Doctor Voodoo).

Nico Minoru

A hereditary witch, the daughter of "dark wizards," Nico Minoru has a magical tool, the Staff of One, with which she can cast virtually any spell—although each spell can only be cast once. Nico must continually dream up new spells. One of the few Japanese-American superheroes, she first appeared in 2003. Nico is the de-facto leader of the Runaways, a group of teenage runaways with superpowers who appear in a Marvel Comics series. Sometimes known as Sister Grimm, Nico has successfully battled Marie Laveau—or at least the Marvel Comics version of her.

The Scarlet Witch

The Scarlet Witch is the code name for Wanda Maximoff, a Marvel Comics superheroine who first appeared in 1964. During her long career, she has been a member of the Avengers, the X-Men, and, in the *X-Men Evolution* cartoon series, briefly a member of the Brotherhood of Evil. Her origins are murky. Over the years, her back-story has evolved and changed, becoming ever more complex. She was originally the daughter of a central European Roma (Gypsy) woman and Magnus the Mutant, who would eventually be conflated with Marvel antihero, Magneto.

Wanda's powers, including the ability to cause spontaneous flames, began manifesting in child-hood. Lacking the knowledge to control them, she causes witch hysteria among local villagers, who seek to destroy the young witch. A mob attacks Wanda and her twin brother, Pietro (the future superhero, Quicksilver), but they are saved by Magneto, who brings them to the United States.

Wanda can magically control probability and change reality. Some consider her to be the most pow-erful character among all the superheroes in the Marvel Universe, but she is emotional and temperamental, leading many readers and Marvel characters alike to consider her a dangerous witch. When some of her fellow superheroes debate killing Wanda, she magically foils them.

Storm

Among the most beloved of all comic superheroines, Storm first appeared in 1975 in the pages of Marvel

Comics. She is among the leaders of the X-Men. Storm, whose true name is Ororo Munroe, controls weather: she raises and calms storms, thus conforming with a medieval stereotype of storm-raising witches.

Storm appears in many different variants of the Marvel Universe. In some, she resembles a goddess; in others, she is explicitly identified as a witch. One of her titles is "The Weather Witch." Storm was among the very first black comic book characters and the first female African-American superheroine. In the *X-Men* movie series, she is portrayed by Halle Berry.

∽⌒○ Tarot: ○⌒∽
Witch of the Black Rose

Making her comic book debut in 2000, Tarot is the star of the Broadsword Comics series named in her honor. The very first issue of *Tarot:* *Witch of the Black Rose* was dedicated to the witches of the world. Tarot's identity as a witch is crucial to the series and its plot.

Tarot stems from a long line of hereditary witches, some of whom were burned at the stake because, in Tarot's words, "they were proud enough to call themselves witches." Tarot, a member of the Black Rose coven, lives in Salem. She is a card-reading, spell-casting witch with a winged, black goblin-cat familiar named Pooka. Tarot is a beautiful, buxom redhead who is usually very scantily clad. The comic series is targeted for mature audiences, not children.

Yuko

Known as the Time-Space Witch, Yuko is the heroine of the Japanese manga series *xxxHolic*, as well as the offshoot anime series of the same name. *xxxHolic* was created by CLAMP, an extremely popular manga-creating team whose members include Nanase Ohkawa, Mokona Apapa, Mick Nekoi, and Satsuki Igarashi. *xxxHolic* first appeared in 2003. As of 2009, the series consists of fifteen books. The series crosses over with another CLAMP manga and anime series, *Tsubasa: Reservoir Chronicle*, in which Yuko also makes occasional appearances.

Yuko is poised, serene, beautiful, exceptionally well-dressed, and mysteriously omniscient. She also has an insatiable appetite for gourmet food and drink. Yuko is the proprietress of a wish-granting shop: she can grant any wish, but for a substantial price. Her familiar is a black butterfly.

Zatanna

A beautiful witch in the guise of a stage magician, Zatanna dresses in a conjurer's top hat and tails, with the addition of fishnet stockings. This DC Comics heroine first appeared in 1964. Her father is an earlier DC character, Zatara. Leonardo da Vinci and Count Cagliostro are among their ancestors. Another relative, the witch Zachary Zatara, first emerged in the pages of DC Comics in 2006 as a member of the superhero team The Teen Titans. Zatanna inherited her father's power to cast verbal spells. She is a member of DC's Justice League.

Famous Witches of Television

Television tends to be a comparatively conservative media, and witches are less prevalent than in books, movies, or video games, perhaps because television is dependent on sponsors to a greater extent than these other forms of entertainment.

Several television programs, however, focus on witches as central characters or feature witches as recurring characters. Audiences have a tendency to become attached to characters that are familiar to them, and the witches described here are no exception. They are extremely beloved characters. In addition to the series discussed here, other programs that prominently feature witches include *The Addams Family*, *Dark Shadows*, *Eastwick*, *Hex*, *Passions*, and the BBC series, *Merlin*.

Dr. Orpheus

The necromancer Dr. Byron Orpheus is among the stars of the American animated television series *The Venture Brothers*, which premiered on Cartoon Network's Adult Swim cable television network in February 2003. Dr. Orpheus first appeared in "Eeney, Meeney, Miney . . . Magic!," the fifth episode of the first season, and has since become a recurring character. He bears a strong resemblance to Marvel Comics supersorcerer, Dr. Strange.

Dr. Orpheus lives on the compound belonging to his landlord, the scientist and former boy adventurer Dr. Rusty Venture. Like Dr. Venture, Dr. Orpheus is a single father—he lives with his teenage-daughter, Triana Orpheus, who is destined to become a great witch herself. Dr. Venture and Dr. Orpheus frequently debate the relative merits of magic versus technology. Although his very first appearance was forbidding, Dr. Orpheus is among the most benevolent characters on the show. Dr. Orpheus repeatedly comes to the rescue of Dr. Venture and his sons, the Venture brothers.

Endora

As played by veteran actress Agnes Moorhead, Endora was initially intended as the villain of the ABC television series *Bewitched*—not because she was a witch, but because she was a mother-in-law. *Bewitched* debuted in 1964, a time when evil mother-in-law jokes were stylish.

Witches are a different species in the *Bewitched* universe, possessing superpowers and only physically resembling mortals, as humans are called. The premise of the show is that Endora's daughter, Samantha, who has fallen in love with and married a mortal, is attempting to live as a mortal, avoiding the use of her magic powers. Endora, who takes tremendous pride in being a witch, is appalled—although she consistently helps Samantha whenever needed. She may disapprove of her son-in-law, but she clearly loves her daughter. Endora is glamorous, tough-talking, and sharp-witted, and is the consistent source of *Bewitched*'s cleverest jokes and lines. She has emerged as a heroine for many 21st-century witches. The name "Endora" references the Bible's Woman of Endor.

The Halliwell Sisters

The Halliwell Sisters are the stars of the WB television series *Charmed*, which debuted in October 1998 and lasted for eight seasons. Three sisters: Prue, Piper, and Phoebe Halliwell, are reunited at their childhood home in San Francisco following the death of their beloved grandmother. The sisters, portrayed by Shannen Doherty, Holly Marie Combs, and Alyssa Milano respectively, are unaware that they are hereditary witches until they discover a massive book in the attic—a true Book of Shadows, containing their family's spells. The book foretells the coming of "The Charmed Ones"—three sister witches who will become the most powerful witches in the world. The sisters soon begin to develop and learn how to control innate superpowers.

The sisters are young, fun, and well-dressed. Despite occasional arguments and hurt feelings, they are exceptionally loyal to each other. The Charmed Ones are protectors of the innocent and enemies of the wicked. Evil forces, especially demons, relentlessly attempt to destroy them and steal their unique, valuable powers.

After three seasons, Shannen Doherty (Prue Halliwell) left *Charmed*, leaving a problematic void. The plot had made it very clear that the power of the Charmed Ones was dependent on their Power of Three. Two sisters were not sufficient to keep the world safe from evil. Enter Paige Matthews (portrayed by Rose McGowan), a previously unknown half-sister who became the third Charmed One. *Charmed* incorporates Wiccan terminology and ritual, although it is a fantasy and does not present realistic depictions of Wicca, witchcraft, or magical practice in general.

Sabrina

The ABC television series *Sabrina the Teenage Witch* features the third incarnation of this character. Sabrina first appeared in October 1962 in the back pages of an Archie comic book. Originally intended as a minor, one-time character, the young blonde witch proved very popular, and by 1971 she was starring in her own comic book series, also called *Sabrina the Teenage Witch*. Following the success of the comic book, Sabrina's second coming, an animated series called *Sabrina the Teenage Witch*, aired on Saturday mornings, debuting in 1971. (A different animated series that hewed more closely to the live-action television series debuted in 1999.)

The ABC television series aired from September 1996 until April 2003. Melissa Joan Hart portrayed young Sabrina Spellman, who goes to live with her aunts Zelda and Hilda, only to discover that they are witches and that she is, too! Much of the series involved Sabrina's comedic adventures as she learned to expand and control her powers and navigate the world of witches while still facing the challenges of any high school or college student. Sabrina's family includes a sardonic, talking black cat named Salem who is actually a transformed witch. Punished by the Witch Council for attempting world domination, Salem is forced to live as a cat.

Samantha Stevens

As portrayed by Elizabeth Montgomery, Samantha is the star of the hit television series *Bewitched*. Samantha is a beautiful, blonde hereditary witch in possession of superpowers—she can accomplish virtually anything merely by wiggling her nose.

Bewitched was a revolutionary program. For the first time, a witch was totally and unambiguously a heroine. She is an extremely sympathetic character—intelligent, kind, sensible, and sensitive. Samantha attempts to juggle the conflicting demands of her beloved husband, Darren, who would like his wife to behave like a regular mortal, and her own family, especially her mother Endora, who find Darren's desires insulting.

Bewitched aired on ABC from September 17, 1964 until July 1, 1972, and then continued to air in syndication. The show was phenomenally popular, holding the record for highest-rated half-hour weekly series ever to air from its debut until 1977. For many viewers, *Bewitched* was the first program to introduce the concept that a witch might be sympathetic. A bronze statue of Samantha was erected in downtown Salem in 2005.

Willow Rosenberg

Willow Rosenberg is the primary witch on the television series *Buffy the Vampire Slayer*, which premiered on March 10, 1997 and lasted for seven seasons. *Buffy* consistently featured themes relating to witchcraft. The third episode of the very first season is entitled "The Witch."

Willow, played by Allyson Hanigan, is Buffy's best friend and advisor. When the series begins, Willow is a shy, awkward, but very smart girl with long red hair. Portrayed as a classic computer nerd, she is delegated to be chief researcher whenever Buffy needs information to help foil marauding vampires and demons. During her quest for esoteric knowledge, Willow becomes a witch—eventually an exceptionally powerful one. Willow is an ambiguous, complex character. Her reliance on magic is used as a metaphor for addiction, with serious consequences for Willow and several other characters.

CHAPTER 7

Animal Witches and Witches' Animals

There are witches' animals, and then there are witch animals. It's a fine but crucial distinction.

Although exceptions exist, witches are legendarily fond of animals. In general, a gathering of magical practitioners will simultaneously be a gathering of animal lovers. During the witch hunt era, one of the alleged tell-tale, sure-fire signs of a witch was someone perceived as too friendly with animals—especially with creatures closely associated with witchcraft and the magical arts like crows, cats, or dogs.

Animals also serve as *familiars*. Familiars are witches' animal companions and partners in magic, assisting in divination, spell-casting, and other magical work. Sometimes the presence of the familiar is sufficient to add a little extra magical zip to a spell or ritual.

The relationship between familiar and witch is characterized by intensely close psychic and emotional bonds. Although hypothetically any creature can be a familiar, some species are considered most likely or most suitable to serve in this capacity. In general, familiars belong to the same species that people commonly keep as pets. Cats, dogs, snakes, and rabbits rank among the most popular familiars.

Witches were once also popularly believed able to transform into the shape of other living creatures. Folktales are filled with accounts of men who, out late at night, are attacked by a vicious beast. The man cuts off the animal's paw, only to discover the next day that a local woman (often someone he knew but didn't suspect, like a wife, sister, maid, or nasty neighbor) is now missing her corresponding hand.

Sometimes, however, the animal itself is the witch. Although this belief exists worldwide, it is especially prevalent in Japan. Certain animals are believed most likely to be witches, like cats, foxes, and snakes. Not every member of one of these animal species is a witch: only a select, magical few. Nor will you necessarily ever encounter these witches in animal form. The most powerful are able to transform into human form, the better to mingle with people and prey upon us. Some tell-tale clues pointing to their true identities do exist, though, and are revealed in the following pages. For simplicity's sake, in *The Weiser Field Guide to Witches*, the word "animal" includes birds and reptiles as well as mammals.

Bats

Comprising almost a quarter of all mammal species, bats are the only mammals that truly fly. (Others, like flying squirrels, just glide.) Wherever bats are found, folklore associates them with witches. Witches are said to ride bats, keep them as familiars, or even transform into them. In other words, those bats you see flying around at night might really be witches in disguise.

Bats are nocturnal. They sleep all day, hanging upside down in large colonies, emerging only at twilight to fly through the air, often in tremendous swarms. These habits correspond to medieval stereotypes of witches, who were also believed to sleep away the day, shirking standard womanly duties, only to emerge at night in roving gangs to fly off to fabulous witches' balls on mountaintops and in forests. Because bats nest deep within Earth, inside caves, caverns, and grottoes, they were also perceived as being privy to Earth's secrets, just like witches.

During certain eras and in some regions, the presence of bats was perceived as a tell-tale sign of a witch. In 1322, Lady Jacaume of Bayonne, France was convicted of witchcraft and burned at the stake. The evidence? Bats were witnessed flying around her house and garden.

 Cats

Cats are the creatures most associated with witches. Although this applies to all cats, the cats *most* associated with witches are black cats. This association may date back to ancient Greece, where Maenads, wild, ecstatic women devoted to the god Dionysus, were believed able to transform into black panthers, among Dionysus' sacred creatures. Witch goddesses Diana, Hekate, and Lilith all sometimes manifest in the guise of black cats.

Black cats are so profoundly identified with witches that they sometimes serve as a kind of symbolic shorthand. In art or photographs, a black cat placed strategically near a woman is used to indicate that she is a witch. The witch doesn't even have to be in the picture—the presence of the black kitty is sufficient to evoke her. A very common Halloween motif is a black cat wearing a witch's pointy hat or seated inside a cauldron. In the animated opening credits of the immensely popular ABC television series *Bewitched*, the heroine witch, Samantha, transforms into a black cat and back. Some advertising posters for the movie, *Bell Book, and Candle* featured a black cat even though the witch's cat in the film is a Siamese.

Black cats, just like witches, evoke powerful reactions. People tend to either love them or fear them. In Britain, black cats indicate good luck, but elsewhere they are associated with bad luck and disaster. Many still believe the superstition that it's bad luck if a black cat crosses your path and will cross a street just to avoid one. That superstition is based on earlier beliefs regarding the true identity of black cats; in many places, black cats were believed to really be transformed witches. It's not a cat that's believed to cause trouble: it's the witch in disguise who's up to no good. During Hungarian witch trials, for example, women were accused of stalking their neighbors in the guise of talking black cats.

Cats were worshipped as holy beasts in ancient Egypt. Bastet, among Egypt's most beloved goddesses, manifested in the shape of a cat or in the form of a cat-headed woman. Bastet, too, had her associations with witchcraft. Among the epithets the Egyptians used to identify her were "The Great Conjuress" and "Mistress of the Oracle."

Cats were also sacred to Norse goddess Freya. Generously feeding feral and stray cats was an old-country technique for staying in Freya's good graces.

Cats would eventually suffer for these associations with witches and goddesses. In 1484, Pope Innocent

VIII issued a decree denouncing cats and their owners. According to this decree, any cat in the company of a woman might be assumed to be a familiar. And if the cat is a familiar, then what is the woman? Pope Innocent commanded that a witch's cats were to be burned with her. He decreed that all "cat-worshippers" be burned as witches. (This was in response to a revival of Freya worship in 15th-century Germany.)

The pope authorized the killing of cats even without an accompanying witch. Cats were captured and burned *en masse*, beginning a vicious cycle: as a result of the decimation of Europe's cat population and people's fear of keeping cats in the home, rats proliferated, leading to an increase in disease, which in turn was blamed on witches, leading to the destruction of still more cats.

In Japan, cats of any color may really be witches. The cat is not a transformed witch: she is the witch. If she is gifted and powerful enough, she may be able to transform herself into the guise of a woman, but the cat is the original and true form.

Not every cat is capable of being a witch. In Japanese lore, only special cat spirits who may be physically indistinguishable from regular cats are witches. (Sometimes the witch cat has distinguishing marks—like a forked tail or multiple tails—but the clever witch may hide them.) The tell-tale sign of a woman who is really a transformed cat witch is that she is completely unable to use dining utensils and can only eat like a cat with her face inside her dish.

Corvid

A family of birds traditionally and almost universally associated with witches, corvids are big, noisy, gregarious, highly intelligent birds with glossy black plumage. Their voices are not mellifluous. Although extremely vocal, they are not songbirds, at least not by conventional standards.

The various members of the corvid family include ravens, crows, jackdaws, and rooks. Magpies are also members of the corvid family, but they are visually distinct from their relatives and possess very different witch associations, so they are considered separately on page 226 Other corvids are so similar that those with an untrained eye may be unable to distinguish between rooks, crows, ravens, and jackdaws.

The Irish Gaelic word *badbh* means both "crow" and "witch" and is also the name of a fierce Irish battle goddess. The black plumage of most corvids matches the traditional attire favored by many witches. Witches are often portrayed in the company of crows in modern Halloween art, but also in such famous paintings as John William Waterhouse's *The Magic Circle* and Henry Meynell Rheam's *The Sorceress*.

Unlike most creatures associated with witches, corvids are not nocturnal, but *extremely* diurnal birds. Crows and ravens greet the sun daily. If you have ever lived in close proximity to them, then you will inevitably have been woken from deep slumber by their raucous cawing at first light. This habit did not save them from negative associations during the witch-hunting era. Because they are black birds who herald the sun's light, the medieval Church associated them with Lucifer, the fallen angel whose name means "light bringer."

Crows are associated with magical deities including Circe, Morgan Le Fey, Nephthys, and Odin. The most famous corvid familiar of all might be Mr. Hotfoot Jackson, Sybil Leek's jackdaw, her constant companion and the star of her 1965 memoir, *The Jackdaw and the Witch*.

Dogs

Incredibly popular companion animals, it's perhaps not surprising that dogs are also popular familiars. Dogs serve as guards, protecting people from spiritual and magical dangers as well as physical ones. British folklore tells of spectral hounds mysteriously appearing to guard, guide, and accompany lone travelers. Once safety is reached, the dog vanishes as mysteriously as it arrived.

Although any dog may serve as a familiar, the dog most closely associated with witches is a black dog. Goddesses Lilith and Hekate traditionally both appear in the guise of black dogs. Witches, too, were believed able to transform into canines. Nicholas Remy (1530–1616), the merciless French witch-trial judge, alleged that women transformed into rabid dogs and wolves. Witch-hunters also claimed that the devil appeared to witches in the form of a black dog. Two dogs were hanged to death in Salem Village, accused of being witches' accomplices.

Some of the most famous historic familiars have been canines: Agrippa's constant companion was Monsieur, his black standard poodle. Mother Shipton kept a black dog of indeterminate breed who accompanied her everywhere.

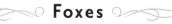 Foxes

Small, wild, and nocturnal, foxes are considered the most feline of canines because of their physical appearance and behavior. (Baby foxes are called "kits.") They are profoundly identified with witches, especially in Japan, where they are the witchcraft animal supreme. Fox goddesses associated with magic and witches are native to China, India, Japan, and Tibet.

In Europe, foxes serve as witches' familiars or as the form into which a witch transforms, but in Japan, some foxes are actually witches. The fox shape is the original form, but a powerful fox witch may be able to transform into the guise of a woman.

Not every Japanese fox is a witch. Most are merely mundane foxes. Lurking among these ordinary foxes are special, magical fox spirits. Fox spirits, known as *kitsune* in Japanese, are characterized by tremendous intelligence and magical prowess. Many fox spirits are gifted alchemists who strive for longevity and immortality. The older the magical fox, the more tails it may possess, although it may not be able to sprout any new tails until it attains one thousand years of age. The most powerful fox spirit is the nine-tailed-fox.

Even without nine tails to identify her, the true identity of a fox witch may be ascertained with close observation. Although a fox witch may resemble a human, there will still be something vulpine about her. Usually her profile will appear snout-like, or she may make fox-like noises. Allegedly, a fox-witch in the form of a woman will cast no reflection in a mirror—or alternatively, her true fox form will appear.

Japanese fox spirits may also serve people as familiars and servants, offering protection and providing wealth. Japan never suffered witch hunts akin to those of Europe or its colonies, but families associated with fox spirits have historically met with discrimination, shunned and feared by their neighbors. (The wealth that fox spirits provide for their loved ones is believed stolen from others.) In Neil Gaiman's 1999 novella, *The Sandman: The Dream Hunters*, a fox spirit works her magic to save the man she loves.

Hyenas

The stereotypical African witch doesn't wear a peaked hat or travel on a broomstick, but she's still a night rider, out journeying to secret assignations with other witches. European witches were accused of riding wolves or bats; African witches ride galloping hyenas, the animals most closely identified with witches throughout Africa.

Hyenas are believed to be a tell-tale sign that will cause someone, usually but not exclusively a woman, to be branded a witch. Any evidence whatsoever, regardless of how flimsy or tangential, that links someone with hyenas may be considered proof of sorcery in African witchcraft trials. These associations are potentially dangerous, as suspected witches are still killed with relative frequency in many parts of Africa.

Folklorically speaking, any hyena may have some association with witches. Witches ride hyenas. Witches keep hyenas, known as "night cattle," milking them daily. In some regions, it's considered dangerous to harm a hyena as its witch will surely magically retaliate. Allegedly, these "hyena cattle" may be identified by the golden earrings they are said to sport.

Witches transform captive victims into hyenas. Witches are hyenas. A talented human witch can transform into the guise of a hyena, the better to creep around at night. Sometimes hyenas are witches. According to Bantu tradition, hyenas are capable of transforming into the guise of humans all by themselves, without the assistance of a human witch. Thus a human may really be a hyena-witch in disguise.

The west African spirit Ogun rides a hyena, indicating his power over witches and witchcraft. He is a great sorcerer—a master of transformational magic—but he can also break any spell or curse cast by a human or hyena witch.

Magpies

Magpies are corvids like their cousins crows, ravens, rooks, and jackdaws, but with their distinctive black and white plumage, they are clearly distinguishable from other corvids. Like their cousins, they are identified with witches, but their mythology is quite different.

Magpies inhabit North America, Europe, north-western Africa, the Middle East, central and east Asia. Despite this wide range, magpies are consistently associated with feminine power, romantic magic, and oracular prophesy. Virtually wherever they are found, magpies are associated with witches—either as their familiars or, more frequently, as the form into which witches transform.

Latvian, Russian, Scottish, and Swedish witches were believed to transform into magpies. Although Siberian witches allegedly possess the power to transform into any creature, folklore says magpies are their favorite choice. A Russian nickname for witch is *soroka-veschchitsa*, meaning "magpie-witch." Various legends describe these magpie-witches. According to one, Ivan the Terrible gathered all the witches he could find in order to burn them, but before this could be accomplished, the witches transformed into magpies and escaped.

Another Russian legend suggests that murdered witches reincarnate as magpies. Although their bodies are those of birds, they retain their witch souls. Since you never know which magpie is a witch magpie, it's crucial to be nice to all of them—otherwise they might cast a spell on you. Some even suggest that when-ever encountering a magpie, one should always salute politely in greeting.

Owls

A particularly ancient species: sixty million years ago, owls were already recognizably owls. Very well distributed, there are extremely few places where owls don't live. Owls inhabit forests, deserts, swamps, plains, and the Arctic region. Wherever they are found, owls are associated with witches. Owls represent sacred yin powers: night, darkness, birth and death, magic, the moon, women and their mysteries.

The Latin word *Strix* and its derivative, *Strega*, literally mean "screech owl," but they're also synonyms

for "witch." Semitic spirit Lilith's name has become synonymous with "witch," but what it really means is "screech owl," too. Owls served as witches' messengers and familiars in ancient Egypt and Rome as well as throughout Asia, Africa, and the Americas. A Madagascar legend says that witches and owls dance together in the graveyard after dark.

Owls are also commonly the guise into which witches transform. That owl one hears hooting late at night might be just a bird—or it might be a witch in disguise. In Lucius Apuleius' 2nd-century AD novel, *The Golden Ass*, the hero watches the Thessalian witch, Pamphile, transform herself into an owl. (When he tries to imitate her spell, he accidentally transforms himself into an ass.) In the 1963 Disney animated film *The Sword in the Stone*, the wizard Merlin takes owl form. In the Rio Grande border area between Mexico and the United States, owls are popularly considered to be transformed witches or witches' allies and messengers.

Pigs

For a variety of reasons, pigs have traditionally been identified with witches, witchcraft, the moon, powerful female deities, and the feminine principle. Reasons may include their affinity for water, their habit of "rooting" in Earth in the manner of a root-worker or herbalist, their identification with fertile, fierce mothers, and, not least, their lunar crescent-shaped tusks.

Sacred sorceress Circe changed men into swine, but pigs and boar, their wild counterparts, are more frequently identified with powerful goddesses and witches than with their transformed victims. Baba Yaga sports boar tusks. Among the spirits depicted as riding pigs are Baba Yaga, Freya, and Isis.

The goddess Cerridwen manifests as a great white sow. Hekate may manifest as a black sow, especially when in an aggressive mood. Black sows are especially identified with witches. Black pigs, especially little fast ones, were traditionally understood to be transformed witches engaged in spell-casting missions. Witch hunters accused witches of offering black pigs to Satan.

On the HBO television series *True Blood*, the mysterious character Maryann first appears in the company of a large, enchanted sow. Pig-witches of a sort appear in Terry Pratchett's *Discworld* novels.

Rabbits

At one time, rabbits and hares were the animals most identified with Europe's witches, playing the role now given to cats. Rabbits serve as witches' familiars and messengers and were believed to be the form into which witches most frequently transform.

The association of rabbits with witches is bittersweet. On one hand, rabbits are the subject of powerful mythology, associated with magic, women's power, and the moon. On the other hand, rabbits, like witches, are often hunted.

Rabbits are very low on the food chain; virtually all predators feast on them. Their survival as a species depends on their fecundity—their amazing ability to reproduce quickly—and on their brains. Rabbits are tricksters, able to hide in plain sight. Wild brown rabbits camouflage well, suddenly appearing and disappearing, as if by magic.

In 1662, Isobel Gowdie, a Scotswoman, apparently volunteered a detailed confession of witchcraft. She described how she and her fellow coven members transformed into hares via a magical chant. English singer Maddy Prior's song "The Fabled Hare" incorporates excerpts from Gowdie's witch trial testimony.

A Devon legend describes how witches congregated after dark on Dartmoor heath. Most people left them alone, but a hunter named Bowerman consistently disturbed them. Finally, enough was enough. One witch transformed into a rabbit. Not realizing her true identity, Bowerman gave chase as she lured him into a magical ambush. Her sister witches surrounded the hunter and his hounds and transformed them into large, granite rock formations that may still be seen on Dartmoor heath.

Witch goddess Hulda is accompanied by an entourage of torch-bearing rabbits. Rabbit witches serve as entertainment for children: in Katharine Pyle's illustrated 1895 children's book, *The Rabbit Witch and Other Tales*, a rabbit witch in a head scarf steals naughty children; in Walter de la Mare's children's poem, "The Hare," "an old witch-hare" gets spooked herself.

The association of rabbits with witches is not limited to Europe. In China, rabbits are identified with witches, alchemy, and sorcery. Instead of a man in the moon, China has an alchemist rabbit in the moon, endlessly grinding the elixir of immortality with his mortar and pestle, a servant of witch goddess Hsi Wang Mu.

Raccoons

Native to the Western Hemisphere and ranging from Canada through South America, raccoons are considered witch animals in many Native American cultures. Solitary, nocturnal, omnivorous, medium-sized mammals, they have dexterous hands, like people.

The raccoon is unique among animals in that, given access to water, it washes its food before eating. Facial markings make raccoons appear as if they are wearing black masks. Their eyes glow at night. Raccoons creep around human habitations at night, searching for food, and although cautious, they display little fear of people. Raccoons are associated, folklorically, with transformation, stealth, and secrecy.

The English word *raccoon* derives from an Algonquin word *arachun*, meaning "the one who scratches himself," but other words for "raccoon" in other Native American languages emphasize associations with witches and magic. In the Cheyenne language, the word for raccoon is *macho-on*, "the one who makes magic." The word for raccoon in Nahuatl, the language of the Aztecs, is *cioatlamacasque*, literally "she who talks with spirits." The Yakima word *tsa-ga-gla-tal* may be translated as witch, spirit, or raccoon.

Snakes

Also known as serpents or vipers, snakes are associated with witches, healers, and practitioners of magic. A Ukrainian word for *witch* also means "snake." Welsh traditions suggest that snakes convene *en masse* on May Eve and Midsummer's Eve—the same nights that witches traditionally revel. Marie Laveau famously danced with a snake during Midsummer's Eve rituals. The legend of Saint Patrick banishing Ireland's snakes is often interpreted as a metaphor for his ejection of magical practitioners.

Snakes serve witches as familiars, companions, and teachers of magic. Sometimes the snakes are witches themselves. In east Asian folklore, powerful serpentine witch spirits disguise themselves as women, enabling them to discreetly blend in to human society.

The Snake-Witch Stone (*Ormhäxan*), a picture stone discovered in a cemetery in Gotland, Sweden, has been dated to approximately the 5th through 7th centuries AD. Picture stones are raised stone slabs embellished with illustrations. The Snake-Witch Stone depicts what appears to be a female snake-charmer with a snake in each hand.

Snakes are associated with divine sorcerers including Angitia, Hekate, Lilith, Ogun, Simbi, and Tlazolteotl. Lilith may appear in the guise of a woman from above the waist and a snake below, while Baba Yaga is sometimes depicted with snakes for legs.

Wolves

The history of wolves and witches runs parallel, as do emotions evoked by them and treatment afforded them. Like witches, wolves have been demonized, hunted, and exterminated. The virulent hostility and determination to exterminate wolves—out of all proportion to any damage they might possibly do or have historically done—parallels emotions toward witches: the urge to kill off something wild, free, independent, and beholden to no one.

In many cultures, links between wolves and witches are very explicit. In the Navajo language, the same word indicates "wolf" and "witch." In the folk traditions of some European Roma (Gypsies), it's important to take magical precautions when a wolf is heard howling, because the sound might really signal the approach of a witch. According to Germanic lore, witches ride wolves. This recalls the Valkyries, ancient Nordic female spirits who also ride wolves. In 11th-century England, the word *Valkyrie* became a synonym for "witch." A wolf is the sacred animal of Italian witch goddess Diana.

Concurrent with the witch hunt era, France suffered a werewolf panic. Men accused of being werewolves were hunted and killed as if they were witches. There is a theory that this werewolf panic—and the conception of werewolves, in general—refers to vestigial Pagan traditions, possibly a society of full moon-worshipping male shamans dedicated to Diana.

CHAPTER 8

Hunting Witches

Fairy tales describe witches luring children into houses constructed of candy and cookies so that they can entrap, enslave, and eat them. Mothers, in days long gone by as well as right now, tell children to behave nicely lest evil witches come to "get" them. The Inquisition accused witches of consorting with Satan and possessing diabolical powers. Many still believe this to be true.

And yet, despite all these fearsome tales, it has historically been the witch who has been persecuted, not the other way around. Witches—or those perceived to be witches—have been hunted, tortured, imprisoned, and murdered. Sometimes the extermination of witches—men, women, and children—was government-sanctioned. On other occasions and still to this day in some places, witches are killed by lynch mobs. These mobs are rarely punished for their actions.

The MGM movie musical *The Wizard of Oz* features a popular song with an extremely catchy, buoyant tune entitled, "Ding, Dong, the Witch is Dead." One might argue that the celebratory song reflects the movie's plot, but renditions of "Ding, Dong, the Witch is Dead" are not restricted to that film. Music boxes playing that tune are available for purchase. Popular singers including Barbra Streisand, Ella Fitzgerald, and Rosemary Clooney have recorded this song. Imagine the scandal if the name of any ethnic group or even the word "woman" was substituted for "witch" in the song's title.

Killing witches is no laughing matter; nor does it occur only in stories, movies, and song. The term *witchcraze* was coined to describe what are also called the Burning Times, a lengthy period in which virtually all of Europe, to greater or lesser extents, as well as European colonies, were buffeted by waves of witch hunting and popular hysteria regarding witches. This era began slowly in the 12th and 13th centuries and peaked in the 14th through the 17th centuries. However, although cases became increasingly rare, legal executions of witches in Europe did not end until almost the end of the 18th century.

The repeal of laws against witchcraft was often unpopular with the masses. When laws were repealed, vigilante justice often took their place. Even now, in the 21st century, witch killings still occur in India and Africa. To this day, witches (or people perceived to be witches) are society's canaries in the coalmine. A good way to judge whether a society is tolerant of its citizens is to see whether witches, and magical practice in general, are permitted, or whether they are suppressed and persecuted. Accusations of witchcraft have also historically been an effective way to remove or eliminate inconvenient people.

The vast majority of those accused or killed as witches are anonymous, but a few very famous women were also touched by the witch hunts.

Báthory, Countess Erzsebet

Popularly known as the Blood Countess, Countess Báthory is rumored to have killed as many as 600 young women. Now often described as the most prolific female serial killer in history, back in the old country she was considered a witch. *Erzsebet*, pronounced *air-zhuh-bet*, is the Hungarian variant of *Elizabeth*. *Báthory* was her maiden name.

Born August 7, 1560, Báthory came from a very elegant, noble, wealthy Hungarian family whose branches extended into Transylvania and Poland. She was the niece of Hungarian-born Stephen Báthory,

Prince of Transylvania and King of Poland. A well-educated woman who was fluent in Latin, Greek, and German as well as her native Hungarian, in 1575, Erzsebet was married to Ferenc Nádasdy, a celebrated Hungarian military hero. As a wedding gift, she received Cachtice Castle, one of his holdings, now in modern Slovakia.

Her husband spent much of his time away at war. While he was away, Erzsebet was left in charge of the local peasants, providing for their needs and policing them as she deemed fit. On several instances, she is known to have intervened on behalf of destitute women. Among her servants was a local witch. Erzsebet or her servants allegedly lured young women to work at the castle, and then proceeded to enslave and kill them in order to use their blood in magic potions to preserve Erzsebet's youthful appearance. The rumor that she bathed in blood does not appear in trial transcripts.

Countess Báthory lived during a tempestuous, transformational time in Hungarian history. Hungary, along with the rest of central and eastern Europe, was engaged in a lengthy, protracted battle with the Ottoman Empire. In addition to fighting over territory and sovereignty, this battle was perceived on both sides as a spiritual war between Christian Europe and the Muslim Ottoman Empire. Erzsebet's husband, Ferenc Nádasdy, earned his reputation battling the Ottomans and was thus considered a Christian hero.

Nádasdy owned vast real estate holdings and was an extremely wealthy man, rich enough to lend the new, cash-strapped king of Hungary a substantial sum. When Nádasdy died in 1604, the king was heavily in his financial debt. The loss of her husband of twenty-nine years caused Erzsebet's finances to suffer. Although rumors had circulated about missing girls for years, it was not until the very end of 1610 that an official investigation was ordered. It is thought possible that Erzsebet, as Nádasdy's widow, may have attempted to collect this debt shortly before her arrest.

On December 30, 1610, investigators arrived without warning at Cachtice Castle. Allegedly, several young female prisoners were discovered there, including one who was dying and one who was already dead. It is unclear how many other bodies were found, but apparently there were many. Erzsebet Báthory was arrested together with four of her servants.

The king sought to charge her with witchcraft as well as murder. Evidence that Báthory was involved in spell-casting was found in the castle. If convicted of witchcraft, all of her substantial property would revert to the crown, rather than to her natural heirs.

However, the powerful and well-connected Báthory family intervened, negotiating with the king. All charges against Erzsebet were dropped. She never stood formal trial, although two hearings were held. Her children retained her property and the king was absolved of all debts he owed to Erzsebet.

The king sought to have Erzsebet executed, but her relatives protested that this would be a family disgrace. Instead, she was bricked up into a suite of rooms in Cachtice Castle, with only an opening large enough for food to be passed to her. She was found dead on August 21, 1614. Several plates of food had gone untouched and it's unknown exactly when she died.

It is very difficult to know whether the accusations against Báthory were true. She may have been the victim of a conspiracy. The king owed her a lot of money. He was a devout Catholic while she was a prominent Protestant. Erzsebet Báthory was never questioned. Her servants were questioned and tortured simultaneously. They confessed to whatever they were asked. Three were executed immediately. Two women were thrown alive into a fire. A male servant was beheaded before burning. The fourth servant was perceived as cooperating with Báthory only under duress, and she was sentenced to life imprisonment.

Beatriz Kimpa Vita, Doña

Doña Beatriz Kimpa Vita was born in approximately 1684 to a wealthy, prominent family in the politically turbulent Kingdom of Congo. Roman Catholic priests and missionaries from Portugal and Italy exerted great political influence in this largely Catholic nation. In the early 18th century, resident Capuchin Fathers encouraged King Pedro of Congo to capture local witches and magicians, as well as those who consulted with them, and sell them as slaves, giving proceeds to the Church.

Beatriz demonstrated psychic capacity in childhood and soon began serving as a spirit medium, joining what the Congolese traditionally considered a benevolent mystical society where she channeled spirits for the benefit of the community. When she married, she retired from the society, but the marriage failed to last. In August 1704, Beatriz suffered an extremely severe illness and then made an abrupt, miraculous, total recovery. She told her father that she had "died," but was now reborn as Saint Anthony of Padua.

Doña Beatriz began to produce miracles, healing the sick and infertile. Witnesses claimed that when she climbed a local mountain, twisted and fallen trees straightened and stood upright in her presence.

A devoted following began to accumulate around her, and Beatriz evolved into a charismatic leader of what her followers considered a mystical Christian movement—although church authorities thought differently.

Beatriz sought to reform the Roman Catholic Church, accusing it of racism and of denying the presence of black saints. While some adored her, Beatriz was also the subject of rumors and accusations of witchcraft. Beatriz was accused of transforming her opponents into beasts, Circe style. Although she claimed to be possessed by Saint Anthony, church authorities counterclaimed that she was really possessed by Satan, and pressured the government to arrest her.

Although publicly claiming to be celibate, Doña Beatriz was secretly in a relationship. She concealed her subsequent pregnancy. Shortly after giving birth in secret, she was captured together with her infant son. Charged with heresy and witchcraft, Doña Beatriz was burned at the stake on July 2, 1706, aged somewhere between twenty and twenty-two years old.

Doña Beatriz reportedly felt that she *deserved* a death sentence, not because of the charges against her but because of her deceptive behavior concerning her pregnancy and her son's birth. Her son was originally scheduled to be burned with her, but at literally the last moment a priest rescued the baby. Doña Beatriz asked that her son be named Antonio after the saint (or herself)—but he was named Jeronimo instead.

Boleyn, Anne

Born in approximately 1507, Anne Boleyn was briefly
Queen of England. King Henry VIII was unhap-
pily married to his first wife, Catherine of Aragon,
who had failed to bear him a male heir. He sought to
marry Anne, whom he was convinced would bear his
son. He petitioned the Vatican to have his marriage to
Catherine annulled, but the Vatican refused. Henry, determined to wed Anne no matter what, began divorce
proceedings, which was extraordinary because Britain
was then a Roman Catholic nation and the Roman
Catholic Church forbids divorce. Henry would break
from the Church in his quest to marry Anne. Henry
and Anne married on January 25, 1533.

Many critics of Henry's actions—and there were many—suggested that he was under Anne's spell, that she had bewitched him in order to become queen. A rumor spread that she had a sixth finger on one hand, considered a witch's mark, which she kept hidden by wearing extra long sleeves.

Anne's first child was not the anticipated son but a daughter, the future Elizabeth I. When Anne's next child was a still-born son, Henry described it as God's punishment on him for consorting with a witch. Anne was arrested on charges of witchcraft and treason based on accusations of infidelity. She was beheaded on May 17, 1536. According to legend, Anne Boleyn haunts her old parish church in the form of a hare.

Franco, Veronica

Veronica Franco was among the most celebrated of what were known as "honest courtesans" (*cortigiana onesta*): well-educated, worldly Venetian women who entertained an upscale clientele (similar to a geisha, rather than a streetwalker). Veronica Franco (1546–1591) was introduced to the trade by her mother, also a *cortigiana onesta*. She hobnobbed with the wealthy, powerful, and influential. Veronica's patrons included some of the foremost men in Venice. She also allegedly had a brief liaison with French king Henri III, whose mother, Italian-born French Queen Catherine de Medici, was reputed to be a witch. The Renaissance master Jacopo Tintoretto painted Veronica's portrait.

Veronica was a gifted poet, publishing books of verse and correspondence—highly unusual for a woman at that time. By the 1570s, she circulated among Venice's most prestigious literary circles. An independent, unmarried, assertive woman, she founded a charity for destitute courtesans and their children.

In 1577, Venice was ravaged by the plague and Veronica left town, as did many other wealthy citizens. When she returned, she discovered many of her possessions missing. She was robbed again in May 1580. This time, she suspected an inside job and began to investigate the crimes.

Veronica Franco was secretly denounced to the Inquisition by her children's tutor, Ridolfo Vannitelli, who, it is suspected, may have been afraid that she would accuse him of theft. She was accused of heresy and engaging in magical incantations.

Venice was among the earliest places in Europe to enact laws against witchcraft. In 1181, the Doge of Venice passed laws prohibiting sorcery. However, in Venice as elsewhere in the principalities that would become modern Italy, witch hunting was mild as compared to other parts of Europe. Although some were executed by burning, most of those convicted of witchcraft in Venice suffered only incarceration, flogging, penances, and banishment. Veronica Franco's was the only trial for magical incantation in 1580.

Franco was accused of conducting a magical ritual involving divination in an attempt to locate her missing goods and identify the thieves. (The ritual was unsuccessful.) She did not deny that this ritual occurred, but told the Inquisition that her neighbors (who may have been suspected of the theft) were the ones who actually initiated and conducted it, despite her own protests. She did also, however, voluntarily tell the Inquisition that she had participated in such rituals as a child.

Veronica's trial records survive. She defended herself admirably before the Inquisition and was not convicted. As an educated woman who traveled in sophisticated circles, she understood the implications of the questions put to her. Friends in high places may have also helped her beat the rap. Although she was not convicted or apparently punished, the social humiliation may have injured her standing in the community. She is believed to have died impoverished in 1591. The 1998 film *Dangerous Beauty* is based on her life.

Gowdie, Isobel

Isobel Gowdie triggered a series of witch trials after allegedly volunteering a confession of witchcraft in Auldearn, Scotland. She testified that she belonged to a thirteen-member coven whose other members she identified to authorities.

Almost nothing is known about Isobel Gowdie other than that she confessed to being a witch on four occasions in April and May 1662. *Why* she would confess is unknown, and one can only speculate as to whether her confession was truly voluntary.

Described as an attractive, red-haired, childless woman who was married to a farmer and lived on a remote farm in Morayshire, Isobel told her interrogators that she used her magic for healing purposes and that she frequently visited the Queen of Fairy, whom she described as the Queen of Elfhame. However, based on surviving testimony, her interrogators were not interested in fairies or benevolent magic spells—they encouraged Isobel to discuss the devil and malicious magic instead.

Isobel claimed that she could transform herself into a rabbit by repeating a charm three times:

"I shall go into a hare,
With sorrow and sighing and little care
And I shall go in the Devil's name
Until I come home again."

A different charm was used to transform back into a woman:

"Hare, hare, God send thee care
I am in a hare's likeness now
But I shall be a woman soon
Hare, hare, God sent thee care!"

Her interrogators demanded that she demonstrate her magical powers, but she was unable to do so, claiming that once she confessed, her powers had vanished. Her confession was confirmed by Janet Braidhead, who Isobel had implicated. No record exists as to the fate of either Janet or Isobel.

Joan of Arc

Born in approximately 1412, Joan of Arc, also known as the Maid of Lorraine, was a young illiterate peasant girl when she emerged from the French countryside to lead French troops to victory against the English and place Charles VII, whom she believed was the rightful king of France, on his throne. She claimed divine guidance and announced that she was on a mission from God.

Joan was victorious, but on May 23, 1430, she was captured by Burgundian forces, who sold her to the English. The bishop who presided over her trial was determined to prove her a witch. If it could be proved that Charles VII had gained the crown of France via witchcraft, then the English could challenge his divine right to rule. Charles did not come to Joan's rescue, even though she was largely responsible for his winning the throne. It's believed that he wished to distance himself from her because he did not wish to be associated with someone many considered a witch.

At her formal ecclesiastical trial, Joan faced seventy charges, among them being a witch, a sorceress, a false prophetess, a diviner, conjurer, and invoker of evil spirits, as well as other charges involving heresy. She was accused of being "given to the arts of magic." Joan represented herself in court against thirty-seven ecclesiastical judges, holding her own with this powerful group of educated men. Most charges could not be substantiated and were dropped. She was finally convicted and condemned to death on only one charge, the wearing of men's clothing. Joan of Arc, aged approximately nineteen, was burned alive at the stake on May 30, 1431.

A question guaranteed to raise hackles, then as now, is whether Joan was or wasn't a witch. Lorraine, the region of France where she was born, bore a reputation for harboring witches and preserving pre-Christian Pagan traditions. It would be among the parts of Europe to suffer especially devastating witch hunts. A century after Joan's death, hundreds of women from Lorraine would be executed as witches.

At the time of her death and for centuries after, it was generally believed by both the French and English that Joan had access to supernatural powers or even possessed them herself. However whether these powers derived from angels as she claimed or whether Joan was a witch was a matter of very heated debate. Joan began to be venerated as an unofficial saint immediately after her death, but she wasn't canonized until May 16, 1920, almost 500 years after her death.

 Tituba

Although she was the third person accused of being a witch in Salem Village, Tituba, an enslaved woman, was the first to confess, perhaps because Reverend Samuel Parris, the slave owner in whose house she labored, beat her until he obtained her confession.

Tituba was from Barbados. All trial documents refer to her as an Indian. Historians believe that she was most likely of Arawak or Carib Indian descent. Her husband was named John Indian. Many assume Tituba to be of African descent, possibly because of widespread assumptions about who was enslaved in the Americas; that Native Americans were also enslaved is comparatively unknown. However, very little is known about Tituba. Author Maryse Condé conjectures in her 1992 novel, *I, Tituba, Black Witch of Salem*, that Tituba was conceived on a slave ship when her African mother was raped en route to Barbados.

What is known is that Tituba entered the Parris household as a teenager and accompanied them to the Massachusetts Colony in 1680, first settling in Boston before moving to Salem Village. The parish home of Reverend Parris was the epicenter of the Salem witch crisis, the point where the witch hunts are considered to have begun.

In addition to Tituba and her husband, John, the Parris household consisted of Reverend Parris, his infirm wife, his eight-year-old daughter Betty, and an eleven-year-old girl named Abigail who is usually described as the reverend's niece, although some speculate that she was actually an unrelated orphan in the family's care.

Salem was a dour, conservative community. No fun or leisure time was permitted, especially not for girls. But during the winter, Tituba entertained the two young girls and their friends with stories while seated in the kitchen, the only warm spot in the house. It is unknown what stories she told.

During the winter of 1691–1692, Betty began to suffer fits and convulsions, which physicians were unable to cure. Rumors spread that she was bewitched. A neighbor, Mary Sibley, recommended the baking of a "witch cake," an English folk magic practice used to determine whether someone was the victim of witchcraft. A cake made of rye and the victim's urine was baked and then fed to a dog. Sibley proposed that Tituba bake the cake, which she did. Her participation in this ritual would later be used as evidence against her.

Eventually, Betty and Abigail accused Tituba of bewitching them. Because she confessed, Tituba was not executed, but was held in jail. Among the first arrested as a witch in Salem Village, she was among the last to be freed.

At the conclusion of the trials, Reverend Parris refused to pay the jailer's fee that was required so that Tituba, his slave, could be let go. As a result, she spent an additional thirteen months in prison until a now-unknown person redeemed her by paying the seven-pound fee. What happened to her after she was released from prison is unknown. Tituba is featured prominently in virtually every fictional depiction of the Salem witch trials, including Arthur Miller's famous play, *The Crucible*. Charlayne Woodard portrays Tituba in the 1996 film version of *The Crucible*, while Gloria Reuben portrays her in the 2003 television movie, *Salem Witch Trials*.

CHAPTER 9

Travel Tips for Witches

Where can you go to learn more about witches? In recent years, several witch-friendly travel destinations have emerged, with sites of interest both to witches and those who are interested in them. In particular, Salem, Massachusetts, the site of the world's most famous witch trials, is filled with places of historical import.

The history of witches stretches back thousands of years. For those who would like to learn more about witches, their craft, and practices, several museums have collections devoted to them.

Castle Halloween

Located in Benwood, West Virginia, Castle Halloween is a museum of supernatural history, housing the personal collection of author Pamela Apkarian-Russell, a renowned authority on Halloween. Its logo features

the profile of a black-hatted witch flying on her broom.
The museum owns over 35,000 Halloween-related
artifacts, including many relating to and featuring
witches, dating from the 1860s to the present. Exhibits
include a section devoted to the Salem witch trials
and an extensive collection of *Harry Potter* memora-
bilia. Castle Halloween is open by appointment only.
Museum website: *www.castlehalloween.com*.

The Museum of Icelandic Sorcery and Witchcraft

Located in Hólmavík, Iceland, this museum is devoted to
traditional Icelandic sorcery and witchcraft as well as the
history of Iceland's 17th-century witch hunts. Hólmavík
is 273 miles north of Reykjavík, in the region of Strandir.
The museum is open between June 1 and September 15,
as well as by special appointment. Museum website:
www.galdrasyning.is.

The Museum of Witchcraft

The world's largest collection of witchcraft-related
artifacts and regalia is housed in Boscastle, Cornwall,
England. The Museum of Witchcraft was founded
by Cecil Williamson in 1951 and originally based
in Britain's Isle of Man. Gerald Gardner was briefly
employed as "resident witch." The museum has been
housed in Boscastle since 1960. Graham King,

the present curator, took over as custodian from Williamson at midnight on Samhain/Halloween 1996. The museum is also home to a library housing over 5,000 occult-related books. Museum website: *www.museumofwitchcraft.com.*

The Museum of Witchcraft Switzerland

Located in Auenstein, Switzerland, approximately thirty miles from Zurich, the Museum of Witchcraft Switzerland (*Hexenmuseum Schweiz*) opened in April, 2009, and features an extensive collection of artifacts, books, and paintings related to witches, folklore, and the practice of magic. The museum is devoted to teaching the truth about modern witches as well as Switzerland's witch hunts. Among the museum's goals is to dispel fear of witches.

Switzerland was among the first regions affected by witch hunting, and among the hardest hit. The Hexenmuseum is an excellent resource for researchers, students, and historians; the museum's curator has scoured the nation's archives, searching for information about this era, and her findings are available at the museum. Guided tours in English are available if booked in advance. More information, in English as well as German, may be found at the museum's website: *www.hexenmuseum.ch.*

Salem

Salem, Massachusetts is America's Witch City. In 1692, Salem Village, in what was then Great Britain's Massachusetts Colony, experienced a wave of witch hysteria. Several young girls claimed to be afflicted by witches. The people they identified as witches were arrested and questioned. Their testimony led to further accusations of witchcraft and more arrests. Salem's witch trials lasted for thirteen months, with accusations levied against 156 people. By the time the witch hysteria ended, nineteen people had been hanged, and one man was pressed to death. People also died while they were imprisoned.

Although the American colonies suffered other witch hunts, none has captured the public imagination as has that of Salem Village. The Salem witch trials are the most famous in the world, and Salem continues to fascinate those who are interested in witches. Ironically, as 17th-century Salem wished to eliminate all possible witches, the economy of modern Salem is largely driven by public fascination with witches.

Salem now has a large resident population of witches and Wiccans. If you are looking for witch stores, Salem has plenty. Many retail outlets sell occult books and the accoutrements of magic, spell-craft, and ritual. Salem offers many museums and places of historic interest associated with witches and the

Salem witch trials. For those interested in the topic, a week's vacation is easily spent in Salem. October is the most popular time to visit, although one can visit any time. October 31, the holiday of Halloween/Samhain, has developed a Mardi-Gras like ambience in Salem, including a three-week Halloween festival, Haunted Happenings, that includes many family-friendly activities. Salem at Halloween/Samhain is a major tourist destination, and hotels are reserved months in advance.

There are actually two Salems: Salem Village and Salem. Most of the events of the Salem witch trials actually occurred in Salem Village, which is on the outskirts of the town of Salem. After the trials were over, the surviving residents of Salem perceived the past events as sordid, scandalous, and shameful. In an attempt to begin anew (or to sweep the scandal under the rug), the name of the original Salem Village was changed to Danvers, as it remains today. However, part of the town of Danvers is now designated the *Salem Village Historic District.* Several sites of interest to witchcraft are located there, including:

- **The Salem Village Parsonage**, the home of Reverend Parris's family and Tituba, the first person in Salem Village to confess to being a witch. This is where the hysteria began.

- **The Witchcraft Victims' Memorial,** dedicated in 1992 to commemorate those who died during

Salem's witch panic. The monument records the names of those who died, as well as final statements by eight of the executed.

+ **The Nurse Homestead**, home of Rebecca Nurse, among those executed for witchcraft, and the Rebecca Nurse Burying Ground, located at the Homestead. Following execution, convicted Salem witches were buried in unmarked graves on Gallows Hill, but Rebecca Nurse's family exhumed her body and reburied her at home.

+ **The Samuel Holten House**, home of Sarah Holten, who testified against Rebecca Nurse.

+ **The Putnam Burial Ground**, resting place of Ann Putnam, one of the "bewitched girls."

Although these historic sites are in Danvers, museums and locations oriented toward students, tourists, and shoppers are found mainly in Salem, including:

+ **The Salem Wax Museum of Witches and Seafarers** depicts the history of Salem Village, from its founding until the end of the witch trials. Fifty life-like wax mannequins set in thirteen tableaux are on display, with Tituba among them. Website: *www.salemwaxmuseum.com*.

- **The Salem Witch Museum** is devoted to the history of the Salem witch trials and is an exploration of the ways in which witches are perceived. The museum recreates the historic witch hysteria via a multi-sensory presentation. Website: *www.salemwitchmuseum.com.*

- **The Witch Dungeon Museum** features a reenactment of a witch trial based on actual trial transcripts and a guided tour of a recreated dungeon. Website: *www.witchdungeon.com.*

CHAPTER 10

Are *You* a Witch?

Are you a witch? That may sound like a simple, straightforward question, but nothing about witches is ever simple. You may already know whether or not you are a witch, but many agonize for years over this question—either because they desire to be a witch or because they fear they are one. Public witches—those who are publicly identified as witches, especially authors, magical practitioners, and proprietors of witch stores—are frequently approached by people seeking affirmation as to whether or not they, too, are witches.

Those who are unsure wonder: how can I be sure? Are there clues or signs?

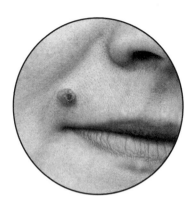

Medieval witch hunters were sure they knew the signs indicating a witch. Some of those alleged telltale signs are now notorious. Witch hunters examined women's naked bodies, searching for a "witch-mark," something that could be construed as physical proof that a woman was a witch. The concept of the witch-mark is nebulous—essentially, whatever a witch hunter chose to see as a witch-mark became one. Possible witch-marks included extra fingers, extra toes, birthmarks or moles, even something as innocuous as a skin-tag.

The notorious "witch's tit" refers to a supernumerary or third nipple, something that modern science suggests occurs in two percent of all women. Witch hunters poked witches with special sharp-pointed tools because they claimed that witches felt no pain. If the woman failed to scream, she was a witch. Even witch hunters didn't believe this fallacy, as some of those tools, now artifacts in museums, were rigged with retracting points. When the tool was pressed against the woman's flesh, the point retracted, causing no pain.

Witches were accused of avoiding salt. You'll know the witch at the table—or so the medieval stereotype went—because she's the one complaining that the food is too salty. This belief may be based on a grain of truth. European fairies notoriously hate salt and will angrily reject any offering containing it. Someone who habitually cooks for fairies—as is customary in some forms of fairy shamanism and witchcraft—will likely become used to avoiding salt.

Witches were accused of lingering in the marketplace, not because they were considered shopaholics, but because witches could allegedly absorb the powerful energy generated by the excitement of negotiations and manipulate this energy for their own benefit. Back in the day, if you spent more time in the marketplace than was perceived necessary, you might have been suspected of being a witch.

Other signs were also believed to identify witches: in cultures where women customarily cover their hair or wear it bound up, witches wear their hair loose. Disheveled, disobedient, or unruly hair is an alleged tell-tale sign of witches. Even if she tries to keep her hair under control, a witch's hair will spring out from beneath a headscarf or refuse to remain in a braid. In old Jewish and Slavic fairy tales, to mention that a woman has disheveled hair is often the tell-tale clue revealing that this character is a witch.

Witches were believed to laugh too loudly and too much. A woman who routinely looked men right in the eye rather than keeping her eyes downcast was also often considered a witch. A relationship with certain types of animals has historically been sufficient to brand someone as a witch, although the type of animal varies depending upon region. The tell-tale animal in much of Africa is a hyena, whereas in Japan, it's a fox. Cats, owls, snakes, and bats are associated with witches virtually wherever those creatures are found.

Those are all medieval or old-fashioned, archaic stereotypes from the perspective of those who fear witches. What do witchcraft traditions suggest? Are there criteria to identify compatriots?

Witches, as you can tell from this field guide, come in a vast variety. There is no one single witch philosophy or belief system; the clues that follow are generalities and not agreed upon by all.

A traditional magical folk belief suggests that those born with teeth or with a caul possess extra magic power. These people may not be witches, but they possess the innate power to become one if they so choose. Many believe that hair indicates magic power. It doesn't have to be messy, unruly, or disheveled, but the hair must somehow be unique or eye-catching either because of its beauty, abundance, unusual color, or something else. In Vodou tradition, babies born with curls are believed to be under the protection of magical snake spirit, Simbi, and may also possess added magic power.

Birth order may indicate potential magical prowess: the seventh son or seventh daughter is famous in folklore as someone with innate charismatic power. The seventh son of a seventh son or the seventh daughter of a seventh daughter is exponentially that many times more powerful.

Here are some further clues to determine whether you are a witch. See if any of these personality traits match your own:

+ You thirst for knowledge and information, especially of a spiritual or magical nature;

+ You have a high tolerance for ambiguity; you're willing to believe that not everything in the universe can be known or proven;

+ You have an affinity for wild nature, a love for the world's wild, untamed places;

+ You're not entirely tame yourself, whether or not anyone else appreciates this about you;

+ You have a fascination with old lore—mythology, folktales, and fairy tales;

+ You identify with the witch, wizard, or sorceress in myth, history, legend, books, or film;

+ You feel a special love or kinship for animals;

+ You are drawn to mystical arts such as astrology, spell-casting, or divination;

+ You possess an independent streak: you don't like being told what you can't do, can't learn, can't know, can't read, or where you can't go.

Any one or more of those clues might indicate that you are a witch or that you could be one if you wanted to be. That may be the most significant clue of all: the desire to be a witch, or the perception that you are one even if you have not yet cast a spell.

Acknowledgments

My thanks to the wonderful people at Red Wheel/ Weiser including Amber Guetebier, Jan Johnson, Michael Kerber, Rachel Leach, Donna Linden, Susie Pitzen, and Sara Gillingham. Heartfelt thanks also to Greg Brandenburgh, Kathleen Cowley, Aline DeWinter, Gwendolyn Holden Barry, Nancy Nenad, and Christopher Penczak.

Further Reading

Books

Bardon, Dr. Lumir and Dr. M.K. *Memories of Franz Bardon*. Salt Lake City: Merkur Publishing, 2004.

Bibbs, Susheel. *Heritage of Power: Marie Laveau-Mary Ellen Pleasant*. San Francisco: MEP Publications, 1998.

Breslaw, Elaine. *Tituba, Reluctant Witch of Salem*. New York: New York University Press, 1997.

de la Mare, Walter. *Down-Adown-Derry: A Book of Fairy Poems*. New York: Henry Holt and Company, 1922.

Drury, Nevill. *Pan's Daughter: The Magical World of Rosaleen Norton*. Oxford: Mandrake, 1993.

Holmgren, Virginia C. *Raccoons: In Folklore, History, and Today's Backyards*. Santa Barbara: Capra Press, 1990.

Illes, Judika. *The Element Encyclopedia of Witchcraft*. London: HarperElement, 2005.

Illes, Judika. *Pure Magic: A Complete Course in Spellcasting*. San Francisco: Weiser Books, 2007.

Illes, Judika. *Encyclopedia of Spirits*. San Francisco: HarperOne, 2009.

Illes, Judika. *Encyclopedia of 5000 Spells*. San Francisco: HarperOne, 2009.

Leek, Sybil. *My Life in Astrology*. Englewood Cliffs, NJ: Prentice Hall, 1972.

Rosenthal, Margaret F. *The Honest Courtesan: Veronica Franco, Citizen and Writer in Sixteenth Century Venice*. Chicago: The University of Chicago Press, 1992.

Thornton, John K. *The Kongolese Saint Anthony: Dona Beatriz Kimpa Vite and the Antonian Movement, 1684–1706*. New York: Cambridge University Press, 1998.

Periodicals

Bennett Jr., Lerone. *"The Mystery of Mary Ellen Pleasant."* *Ebony Magazine*, June 1993, Volume 48, Number 8.

Internet Sources

The **Black Hat Society Network** is an eclectic and private Pagan social organization that welcomes witches, Wiccans, shamans, Druids, and magical practitioners of all kinds. Local chapters meet monthly for socializing, friendship, and discussion, as well as to organize events including art shows, charity events, Sabbat celebrations, circles, and festivals. More information: *www.myspace.com/blackhatsocietynetwork.*

The **Goddess Aradia and Other Subjects** is an extensive website that focuses on Aradia and ancient and modern witchcraft with an emphasis on Italian traditions. The site includes much historical information as well as spells and recipes gathered by author Myth Woodling. More information: *www.AradiaGoddess.com.*

My Hoodoo Space is an online social networking site for conjurers, spiritual workers, eclectic sorcerers, and witches, too. It is a place to form friendships, chat, share spells, and announce events. African Diaspora traditions are emphasized, although not exclusively. More information: *myhoodoospace.ning.com.*

Winterspells: A Magical Life in Faery Witchcraft is a place to explore and develop your own magical personality. Author Aline DeWinter's blog features a magical library as well as lessons and tutorials in Faerie Witchcraft. More information: *www.winterspells.com.*

About the Author

Judika Illes fell in love with witchcraft and the magical arts as a child and has been studying them ever since. Her interests include tarot, runes, and other forms of divination, astrology, spell-casting, traditional healing and spirituality, Kabbalah, the Egyptian Mysteries, mythology, folklore, and fairy tales. Judika served on the tutorial staff of the Australasian College of Herbal Studies. She wrote the popular monthly feature "Beauty Secrets of the Ancient Egyptians" for Tour Egypt, the Egyptian Ministry of Tourism's online magazine. Judika is the author of *Pure Magic, Magic When You Need It, The Element Encyclopedia of 5000 Spells, The Element Encyclopedia of Witchcraft,* and *the Encyclopedia of Spirits*. She lives in New Jersey.

To Our Readers

Weiser Books, an imprint of Red Wheel/Weiser, publishes books across the entire spectrum of occult and esoteric subjects. Our mission is to publish quality books that will make a difference in people's lives without advocating any one particular path or field of study. We value the integrity, originality, and depth of knowledge of our authors.

Our readers are our most important resource, and we appreciate your input, suggestions, and ideas about what you would like to see published. Please feel free to contact us to request our latest book catalog, or to be added to our mailing list.

Red Wheel/Weiser, llc
500 Third Street, Suite 230
San Francisco, CA 94107
www.redwheelweiser.com